Perfecting the Dance

Perfecting the Dance

Soulful Lessons about Love, Faith, and Courage

Nesha L. Jenkins-Tate, Ph.D.

BALBOA
PRESS
A DIVISION OF HAY HOUSE

Copyright © 2015 Marnishia L. Jenkins-Tate.

All rights reserved. No part of this book may be used or reproduced by any means, graphic, electronic, or mechanical, including photocopying, recording, taping or by any information storage retrieval system without the written permission of the publisher except in the case of brief quotations embodied in critical articles and reviews.

On the book cover is the commissioned painting, **Perfecting the Dance**, by Reina Cottier of Reina Cottier Art. Copyright © 2014 transferred to Marnishia Jenkins-Tate.

Balboa Press books may be ordered through booksellers or by contacting:

Balboa Press
A Division of Hay House
1663 Liberty Drive
Bloomington, IN 47403
www.balboapress.com
1 (877) 407-4847

Because of the dynamic nature of the Internet, any web addresses or links contained in this book may have changed since publication and may no longer be valid. The views expressed in this work are solely those of the author and do not necessarily reflect the views of the publisher, and the publisher hereby disclaims any responsibility for them.

The author of this book does not dispense medical advice or prescribe the use of any technique as a form of treatment for physical, emotional, or medical problems without the advice of a physician, either directly or indirectly. The intent of the author is only to offer information of a general nature to help you in your quest for emotional and spiritual well-being. In the event you use any of the information in this book for yourself, which is your constitutional right, the author and the publisher assume no responsibility for your actions.

Any people depicted in stock imagery provided by Thinkstock are models, and such images are being used for illustrative purposes only.
Certain stock imagery © Thinkstock.

Print information available on the last page.

ISBN: 978-1-5043-2913-2 (sc)
ISBN: 978-1-5043-2915-6 (hc)
ISBN: 978-1-5043-2914-9 (e)

Library of Congress Control Number: 2015903566

Balboa Press rev. date: 03/17/2015

*This book is dedicated to you
for all that you are and all that you do
as one of several billion dancers on this planet
that we share.*

*It also is dedicated to the One
who lends breath and guidance
to every dance.*

Brief Table of Contents – Chapters

Introduction: *To Learn, to Love, to Serve* xvii

PART ONE: Practicing the Dance 1

    1. People-Pleasing 3
    2. Parenting 21
    3. Friendship 43
    4. Soul-Searching 61

PART TWO: Performing the Dance 79

    5. Partnering 81
    6. Love-Lessons 95
    7. Setting Love Free 119
    8. Forgiveness 137
    9. Happiness 157

PART THREE: Perfecting the Dance 175

    10. The Purpose inside Your Soul 177
    11. The Language of New Leaders 203
    12. The Soul of a Woman 223
    13. The Choreographer of 7 Billion Dancers 237

Epilogue: *Writers' Woes* 257

Afterword 259

About the Author 263

Detailed Table of Contents – Lessons

Introduction xvii

PART ONE: Practicing the Dance 1

Chapter 1   People-Pleasing 3

Lesson 1:   Me, My Soul, and I 5
Lesson 2:   Give and Let Give 6
Lesson 3:   Take a Load Off 8
Lesson 4:   Know the Power of "No" 9
Lesson 5:   Beware of the Glory-Grabbers 11
Lesson 6:   Digging for Dirt 13
Lesson 7:   Permission Granted 14
Lesson 8:   Affirmation: I am Enough 15
Lesson 9:   Affirmation: I am a Resource 17

Chapter 2   Parenting 21

Lesson 10: Dwell on the Things They Do Well 23
Lesson 11: Don't Create Holes in your Child's Heart 23
Lesson 12: A Solid Foundation for Communication 26
Lesson 13: Respecting the Power of Love 35
Lesson 14: Children only Lie when the Truth Hurts 36
Lesson 15: Seeing through Weeds & Planting Seeds 37
Lesson 16: Tricycles 38
Lesson 17: Let your Children See You Dancing 40
Lesson 18: Meditation: Pray over your Nest 41

Chapter 3   Friendship 43

Lesson 19: Friends Allow Us to Breathe 45
Lesson 20: Love Needs Trust and Trust Needs Truth 46
Lesson 21: Your Bliss is a Blessing Worth Sharing 47

Lesson 22: Don't be Jealous, be Zealous..........................49
Lesson 23: Watch your Watchers................................50
Lesson 24: Click "Aloof" and Poof—It's Canceled!............51
Lesson 25: Life is a Drama..53
Lesson 26: Standing in the Gap 54
Lesson 27: Your Waters Washed my Wounds...................56
Lesson 28: Affirmation: I am a Witness.........................57

Chapter 4 Soul-Searching 61

Lesson 29: Soulitude 63
Lesson 30: You are in the Making 63
Lesson 31: Trust your Intuition...................................64
Lesson 32: A Declaration of Interdependence...................65
Lesson 33: Anger, Fear and Sadness 67
Lesson 34: How Wide is your "We?" 70
Lesson 35: Stick a Fork in It......................................71
Lesson 36: Shake Things Up! 72
Lesson 37: What's on the Spine of your Book of Life? 74
Lesson 38: Your Life is a Glorious Dance!......................75
Lesson 39: Affirmation: I am Letting my Guard Down 76
Lesson 40: Affirmation: I am Opening Up......................76

PART TWO: Performing the Dance................................79

Chapter 5 Partnering..81

Lesson 41: Let's Love Fearlessly.................................83
Lesson 42: Awakened by the Music 83
Lesson 43: A Sweetness that is Completeness.................84
Lesson 44: I Want an Extraordinary Love......................85
Lesson 45: How Do You Recognize Love?......................86
Lesson 46: May We Dance?.......................................88
Lesson 47: Please Teach Me How to Twist 89
Lesson 48: I am Listening to your Heart.......................89

Lesson 49:	Finding that Missing Peace	90
Lesson 50:	Having Faith in Fate	91
Lesson 51:	Waiting to be Wooed by a Lion	92
Lesson 52:	Affirmation: I am on the Wings of Love	93

Chapter 6 Love-Lessons 95

Lesson 53:	How the Milk Man Saved Her Life	97
Lesson 54:	Observe what is Served before You	97
Lesson 55:	Sending Mixed Signals	98
Lesson 56:	What We Fear may be What We Attract	100
Lesson 57:	Her Story	101
Lesson 58:	His Story	102
Lesson 59:	Holding a Story Together	103
Lesson 60:	Mr. Asset, Meet Ms. Accessory!	103
Lesson 61:	Love's Trilogy through Pain	106
Lesson 62:	Too much Passion can be a Poison	107
Lesson 63:	When Opposites Attract	108
Lesson 64:	Time for the Changing of the Guard	108
Lesson 65:	Rearranging the Rooms in Your Heart	110
Lesson 66:	Finders, Keepers, Rulers, Weepers	112
Lesson 67:	Center Yourself in Love	115
Lesson 68:	Wait for the One who Sees You	116
Lesson 69:	Surrender your Heart, Never your Soul	116
Lesson 70:	Affirmation: I am Growing in Love	117

Chapter 7 Setting Love Free 119

Lesson 71:	Breathing in a New Life	121
Lesson 72:	Beyond the Bridges	121
Lesson 73:	Broken	122
Lesson 74:	Love Cannot be Convinced	123
Lesson 75:	Incompatible	123
Lesson 76:	Mine ALL Mine	124
Lesson 77:	Loving while Leaving	126

Lesson 78: Slow-dancing with the Shadows 127
Lesson 79: Abandoned Dreams and Broken Bonds......... 127
Lesson 80: God, is that You Talking or Me? 129
Lesson 81: Bridges, Boardwalks and Cliffs 131
Lesson 82: Set Stuff Free!.. 131
Lesson 83: Affirmation: I am Giving and Letting Go 132
Lesson 84: Affirmation: I am Kissing the Sun................... 134
Lesson 85: Affirmation: I am Whole 135

Chapter 8   Forgiveness... 137

Lesson 86: My Tears are Prayers.................................... 139
Lesson 87: Forgive until You Forget 139
Lesson 88: Blocking Arteries... 140
Lesson 89: Who do You Trust? 140
Lesson 90: Feeding a Grudge, Starving Your Soul 142
Lesson 91: Lifting the Veil 143
Lesson 92: Dance Lessons 144
Lesson 93: When Bullies Grow Up: Recovery Steps........ 145
Lesson 94: Thief in the Night... 150
Lesson 95: Forget to Forgive but Remember to Live........ 151
Lesson 96: Meditation: Thanks for Forgiveness 152
Lesson 97: Meditation: Prayer for a New Day 153
Lesson 98: Affirmation: I am Built for Love 154

Chapter 9   Happiness 157

Lesson 99: Dancing with Life as It Comes Your Way 159
Lesson 100: Fuel for Every Journey 159
Lesson 101: Taking Chances 160
Lesson 102: Healing a Homesick Soul............................... 161
Lesson 103: I only Fear my own Despair 162
Lesson 104: Hope is your Light 163
Lesson 105: A Hunger for Love 164
Lesson 106: Built and Born to Thrive 165

Lesson 107: Old Age Loves a Sage 167
Lesson 108: Affirmation: I am One of God's Fruits 168
Lesson 109: Affirmation: I am Touched 169
Lesson 110: Affirmation: I am Affirming Life 170
Lesson 111: Affirmation: I am Renewed 171
Lesson 112: Affirmation: I am Still 171
Lesson 113: Meditation: Playing your Song 172

PART THREE: Perfecting the Dance 175

Chapter 10 The Purpose inside Your Soul 177

Lesson 114: Wake-up Call 179
Lesson 115: Listen to your Calling 179
Lesson 116: Purpose, Destiny, Choice and Chance 180
Lesson 117: Be the Main Character in your Story 189
Lesson 118: Your Vision or your Television? 190
Lesson 119: Don't Block your Blessings 191
Lesson 120: Living with Balance is a Challenge 191
Lesson 121: How Badly do You Want It? 193
Lesson 122: Forging Signatures 195
Lesson 123: Beyond Your Dreams 196
Lesson 124: Affirmation: I am Humbled 197
Lesson 125: Affirmation: I am Singing on Purpose 198

Chapter 11 The Language of New Leaders 203

Lesson 126: A Greater Good 205
Lesson 127: Leaders Follow Leaders 205
Lesson 128: Standing Center Stage 206
Lesson 129: Optimist, Pessimist, Realist, Catalyst 207
Lesson 130: Who do You Think You are? 209
Lesson 131: You are a Promise 210
Lesson 132: What Works at Work won't Work Here 210
Lesson 133: Take the High Road 215

Lesson 134: 12 Lessons Great Leaders Learn 216
Lesson 135: Affirmation: I am Greatness 220

Chapter 12 The Soul of a Woman 223

Lesson 136: Glorious is your Testimony 225
Lesson 137: Know your Worth 225
Lesson 138: Guardian of God's Fruits 226
Lesson 139: Maternal Love is Eternal Love 227
Lesson 140: A Peace of Her Soul 228
Lesson 141: May You Dance, Dr. Maya 229
Lesson 142: V Stands for Woman 230
Lesson 143: Little Ms. BaddAzz 230
Lesson 144: Meditation: Ain't too Proud to Pray 232
Lesson 145: Affirmation: I am a Soldier 234

Chapter 13 The Choreographer of 7 Billion Dancers ... 237

Lesson 146: 7 Billion Pieces of God's Heart 239
Lesson 147: Falling on my Face and into Grace 240
Lesson 148: Ordering Your Footsteps 243
Lesson 149: Many Seekers, Many Paths, One Destiny 244
Lesson 150: Pressing toward a Higher Mark 245
Lesson 151: Grieving the Loss from a Gold Mine 245
Lesson 152: All that Ever Is 247
Lesson 153: Same Blood 248
Lesson 154: Our Race toward Disgrace 249
Lesson 155: Words Unheard by the Elephants 250
Lesson 156: Meditation: Prayer of Humility 252
Lesson 157: Perfecting the Dance 253

Epilogue 257

Afterword 259

About the Author 263

Acknowledgments

I am thankful to God—for everyone and everything.

I am thankful to many thought-leaders, teachers, scholars, poets, philosophers, pastors, scientists, and sages. All have enlightened my vision and lent depth to my understanding.

I feel blessed to have meshed with New Zealand's wonderful abstract artist, Reina Cottier, who was inspired to paint the beautiful commissioned artwork on the cover.

I am thankful to my ancestors and my grandparents in the heavens—Fred and Wilhelmena Jenkins, and Esau and Janie Jenkins—for honoring my creative spirit as a child and for encouraging me to be a brave voice.

I am grateful to Ms. Flo Myers, our family's matriarch. Regal, loving and trail-blazing, she is a lioness who has taught me the true dignity of self-love.

I am grateful to my parents, James and Alfreda Jenkins, who recognized early talents in each of their children, and then inspired us to have the courage to serve our purpose with a spirit of love and conviction. I also thank my parents for being encouraging creative consultants over the course of this project.

I am grateful to my brothers—Manotti, Maurice and Melvin—for being not only my siblings but sometimes also my fraternal soul-mates.

I am grateful to my son, Kahlil Masai Tate, who came into this world a very old soul, instinctively wise about soulful things. He is a young man now in pursuit of his own calling, and I hope that he will share this book forward as an heirloom of my heart.

I am grateful to my sons, Malik and Zuri, and to my daughters, Lisa and Tahara, who came here through kind moms who have allowed me to share their love. They taught a young step-mom how to be a grateful parent and a graceful human being.

I am thankful for my godmother, Veronica Rogers, who is my first best friend ever.

I am thankful to family and friends who encouraged my writing—and who were patient with my distance many evenings and weekends as I labored to give birth to this book.

I am grateful for those with whom I share worship and fellowship at Crossover Church, especially my niece, Azania Jenkins; and for the soul-sustenance and guidance of Pastor Timothy Seay.

I am grateful to the men who have been among my closest friends, mentors and muses—especially George Tate, Charles Brooks and David Burns.

I am thankful to the thousands of friends, fans and followers who support my daily inspirational blog at *Lovepoems4peace by Dr. neeesh*.

Introduction

To Learn, to Love, to Serve

I believe, most fundamentally, that we come to this earth as human beings to learn, to love, and to serve. And the soulfulness of dance offers the most powerful living metaphor for capturing the essence of those experiences.

The dance, as referenced across these pages then, speaks to how we do those things—learning, loving and serving—as we interact moment-by-moment with ourselves and with each other. After all, our relationships are the core connections that help us to define who we are as human beings.

So this book is offered to you in three parts. The chapters in Part One, *Practicing the Dance*, focus on the relationships that lay the foundation for lifelong learning. Part Two, *Performing the Dance*, explores relationships and situations that most expand our capacity for loving. And Part Three, *Perfecting the Dance*, suggests ways that relationships can offer us opportunities to be instruments of service.

So this isn't a book about perfection. It is a book about *perfecting*—constantly discovering new ways to approach the twists and turns, the highs and lows, the breaks and flows of life—while being guided by love, faith and courage.

Dr. Nesha Jenkins-Tate

And this isn't a book about perfecting the dancers. It is a book about perfecting the *dance*—navigating the continuous life-loop of change, pain, healing, transformation, and the acceptance of a new normality—which, over time, will evolve into more cycles of change.

This is an inspirational book steeped in spirituality. It pays homage to the interior-life that grows and sustains the human spirit and that often informs and guides our exterior-life.

Thus, this book is as much a love-offering to our Supreme Being as it is anything else, whether we are moved to call that supreme force by the name—Abba, ALL, Allah, Almighty, Bahá, Brahman, the Creator, Dios, Divine Goddess, Elohim, God, Grace, Great Mother, Great Spirit, Hu, The Great I Am, Jehovah, Jesus Christ, Krishna, the Light, the Lord, Love, the One, the Universe, Yahweh, the Divine—or some other sacred and all-powerful name that has held human beings in Faith across time.

Most often, this book refers to that divine force as God. Many times God is referenced by the masculine pronouns, *He* and *Him*, and the masculine adjective, *His*. However, I do believe that God encompasses and embraces all genders and all people; and that God flows through everything that lives and all that ever is.

And I believe the Creator loves us all—the believers, non-believers, agnostics, seekers, atheists, monotheists, polytheists, and whatever else have you. He embraces us all, recognizing our beauty and our baggage; seeing beyond our hypocrisy, our skepticism, and even our overzealousness; and understanding the limitations of our understanding, since we are, by His own design, merely human.

Perfecting the Dance: Soulful Lessons about Love, Faith and Courage isn't a storybook or a novel, so it needn't be read in chapter order.

It is a collection of candid, practical life-lessons learned on a journey that has been sustained by love, faith and courage. It is a compilation of over 150 selected essays, testimonials, affirmations, poetry, prose, prayers and epiphanies—clustered by themes across 13 chapters. And each chapter addresses a general topic that is relatable in some way to all who share the human experience.

This book is an easygoing companion of sorts, so have fun with it. It allows you to engage with it in the manner that feels most resonant and convenient for you in any given moment. To illustrate some of the many ways you can choose to engage with it, consider the following:

You can sip it like a tea ritual. Allow the book to be your daybook or your weekly-reader. There are over 150 lessons across 13 chapters. Try reading one lesson per day in sequence over the course of five months. Or, try focusing on one chapter per week, incorporating some of the lessons in your daily living, over the course of three months.

You can let it quench your immediate thirst. Select the chapter-theme most relevant to your life in this moment and fully indulge the moment with the collection of readings on that topic. Make notes about your own insights and feelings and create an action plan in the notes section at the end of each chapter.

You can roll the dice and leave it to chance. Each reading is numbered in the table of contents. So randomly pick a number (between 1 and 157) and allow that corresponding lesson to be your special message for the moment. Make a game of it, engaging a friend by selecting and reading random selections to each other.

You can explore for things that pique your curiosity, and then dig deeper. Browse through the lessons in the detailed table of contents and pick the titles you find most intriguing. Then expand your discoveries from there. Make it a soul-searching adventure.

You can augment your daily devotional readings. At the end of each chapter are affirmations and meditations, about 25 of them in total. Perhaps you'll find some that you like enough to incorporate into your daily meditative readings.

You can make it a group activity. If your book-club, couples-club, classmates, or circle-of-friends decide to read the book, consider assigning each of the three main parts as a topic over three separate sessions. Each part of the book is comprised of four to five short chapters and your meeting host can even create a "lesson plan" for the group, selecting and assigning topics and lesson-numbers. And here's another idea: when you meet for group-discussion, don't forget to infuse some music and group dancing! It's the perfect, fun way to embrace and celebrate the true spirit of *Perfecting the Dance*.

And of course, you can engage in the traditional way. You may simply choose to read it as most of us read most books—in solitude, from cover-to-cover, reminded of all the many lessons that you, too, have discovered on your life's journey along the way.

However way you choose to read it and however often, I do hope that *Perfecting the Dance* will serve as a source of inspiration for you. May it resonate on many days in many ways with your soul. And may it be an intimate companion that whispers to your heart when you need it, making it clearly known—that on this life's journey, none of us ever dances alone.

So, enjoy the dance.

PART ONE

Practicing the Dance

*There is a loving tone of voice
and a careful choice of words that we'd use
while correcting a child who has made a mistake.
More often we should practice speaking to ourselves
in that same way when we make mistakes.*

*Remember that you are a growing child of God,
prone to an occasional misstep or misturn.
So be gentle with your own heart
as you learn.*

*As you learn, teach. As you teach, grow.
That is how we learn what we still don't know.*

Chapter 1

People-Pleasing

*People who are users will chew you up,
spit you out, and then walk away
while complaining about how you got stuck
between their rotting teeth.
So never train a taker to become a user—
a user who becomes an abuser.
Know when you've given enough.
And stop.*

*Never allow a coward to grow courage
by feeding on your fears.
Stand brave. Stand tall.
You were built to play fair,
not built to play small.*

Chapter 1
People-Pleasing

Lesson 1:   Me, My Soul, and I
Lesson 2:   Give and Let Give
Lesson 3:   Take a Load Off
Lesson 4:   Know the Power of "No"
Lesson 5:   Beware of the Glory-Grabbers
Lesson 6:   Digging for Dirt
Lesson 7:   Permission Granted
Lesson 8:   Affirmation: I am Enough
Lesson 9:   Affirmation: I am a Resource

Lesson 1:
Me, My Soul, and I

Sometimes it's not about what's good or bad; right or wrong; weak or strong.

Sometimes it's just about being true to what's inside you. It's remembering that you have the right to choose how you show-up in your own life.

Often we can wrap ourselves so tightly in the heavy garments of roles, rules, goals and social conformity that we suffocate ourselves and lose touch with our core essence.

It is equally easy today to allow ourselves to be absorbed by an overload of noise and sensory stimulation. But at what cost? Eventually we start to feel inwardly disconnected, distracted, scattered and lost—constantly and compulsively wired to respond and react to the whims of the world.

So that is why you sometimes have to make the time to quietly and gently repossess and caress the core of your soul. Carve out spaces where you can feel free—to just quietly, deeply, and authentically be. Get re-centered in your soul.

Alone, on your own, seek the highest guidance. Whisper the things you need to confide. Listen. Observe. Breathe into the moment. Smile at what moves you deeply inside.

And then, perhaps Divine answers will begin to clearly and carefully unfold—because only the truest you can re-awaken to the Whisperer who lives in your soul.

Dr. Nesha Jenkins-Tate

Lesson 2:
Give and Let Give

Some of us are just naturally givers. We give easily because there is something inside us that compels us to be kind, to share joy and love with others.

But some of us are perpetual givers.

Maybe we've learned that we can earn love by being useful to others. Maybe we've always had enough to spare because we don't like being in the position of needing help. Or maybe it just makes us feel favored to give to those who don't have what we have.

And there can be a love-hate dynamic between perpetual givers and perpetual takers.

Loving that you give it, but resenting that you've always got it to give. Loving that you are self-sufficient and never need anything from me, but resenting that what I have to offer seems worth nothing to you.

A useful giver can actually train a taker to feel entitled to the kindness of others.

But people who are "users" will chew you up, spit you out, and then walk away while complaining about how you got stuck between their rotting teeth. So never train a taker to become a user—a user who becomes an abuser who feels entitled to your kindness. Know when you've given enough. And stop.

Especially if you are a perpetual giver, maybe it's time to teach yourself and those around you how to give to you. How?

Perfecting the Dance

Simply relax, and rely on other people sometimes. Allow others—your children, partner, parents, siblings, friends, and colleagues—to know that you need them to be there for you sometimes, too.

And when they offer help, take them up on it. Resist the temptation to refine what they give to you. Swallow the compulsion to return the favor. And humble yourself with a show of gratitude.

Learn to put up your feet and open your hands sometimes, because no matter how much joy you get from giving to others, sometimes the best thing that you can give to others is the opportunity to give to you.

Moreover, recognize that trying to accommodate all the demands of your life and all the demands of your loved ones will leave you in a constant state of being overwhelmed. With too many hands tugging at your heart, you will feel pulled in several directions all at once, with nothing left inside as a center for nurturing yourself.

So learn to get quiet and throw up your hands sometimes—not as a gesture of defeat but as a gesture of surrender to the will and the guidance of your Faith.

Acknowledge that you cannot be all things to all people and that your hands alone can't fix everything that goes wrong. Acknowledge that you actually are depriving others when you don't allow them to learn that oftentimes they can rely on themselves. Acknowledge that sometimes they simply may need to build a relationship with their own Faith instead of relying on you to serve as their almighty.

So your lesson, perhaps, is twofold. Learn to allow others to give to you. And learn to lend a loving hand only when you can—understanding that sometimes all you will need to lend are merely "praying hands," asking God to stand with those you love to help them grow, hoping they will know just how much you love them still.

Life can feel more balanced when we've learned how to give and take. It completes the cycle of giving, and it teaches us the wisdom of long and graceful living.

Lesson 3:
Take a Load Off

Long after the so-called strong people
have been worn down or they're finally gone—

All those so-called weak people will still be here,
managing somehow to keep carrying on.

So God does not ask us to be "all-purpose."
We are simply asked to be "on purpose."

That's it.
And that's enough.
So there's no need to always be
the dumping ground for everyone else's stuff.

Life is bigger than constant battles,
struggles and strife.
So take the load off your shoulders,
and reclaim the joy in your life.

Lesson 4:
Know the Power of "No"

Even babies instinctively recognize the power of the word—*No!* There is a proud defiance in their posture when they recognize that they have the power to reject things they don't want in their space.

Isn't it a pity that, as we grow up, we forget that sometimes?

Observe the thing about which you find it most difficult to say no. Note the thing from which you find it difficult to walk away when it is offered to you.

Is it money? Food? Sweets? Sex? Alcohol? Drugs? Is it more and more work and responsibility? Is it any request made of you by your children? Is it anything that comes to you packaged as "free"?

Whatever that thing is, it is a weakness that can throw you off balance and it can cause you to fall. If you struggle with saying no to a thing, then that thing is your struggle.

And over time, it can evolve itself into cravings, obsessions, or addictions that ultimately become the primary composition of your life. It has the power to steal joy and beauty from your destiny.

So start today, start now, to take your power back from that thing. But how?

If it is fundamentally a good thing but you have a problem of abusing it, learn to set boundaries so you have a conscious sense of what is enough, because somewhere in the word *enough* is the word—*no*. Look at new ways that you can channel the thing toward its highest good. For example, if you can't say no to food, gather food or prepare food and re-distribute it to those who have little or no food.

But if there is no redeeming value to the thing, and quite often that is the case, condition your mind to see the thing as foreign or harmful to you—because it is.

Visualize it literally eating at you, corroding your essence, like a million fat, hungry maggots. And take action to relieve yourself of the parasites.

You may need to reject the thing from your life in every form. Stop giving it the safe harbor of secrecy where it can continue to nibble on you as you provide cover. Shine light on it by being honest about your struggle and asking people who love you to support your walk toward freedom. Seek a support group.

Stay away from the people and places that enjoy seducing you and reducing you by producing for you the very things that they know will make you feel weak. Walk away, and stay away, from predators who seek your company solely because they are addicted to stealing your power and depleting your soul.

Anything to which you cannot say no is likely a negative influence. It will compromise your positive influence in the lives of others and even your ability to influence yourself toward wise decisions.

It will steal even the love you have for yourself.

God is the giver of life, the source of our power. And only the Creator should have that kind of power in our lives—the power to compel us to say *yes* every time to life.

Lesson 5:
Beware of the Glory-Grabbers

Don't you just love the glory-grabbers? They are the people who rush in just as things are looking bright and promising in your life, and they seem to try to single-handedly snatch away your joy.

It's usually not in obvious or direct ways but through passive-aggressive, "make nice" comments. So it's difficult to call them on it, but it's easy to feel the impact of the sting.

As is true of many writers and artists, I was born with a thin-skinned, porous sensitivity that is both a gift and a curse. So I am particularly attuned to glory-grabbers. They get under my skin even as I know better than to let them in. And shucks, truth be told, I even might be guilty of having done some glory-grabbing myself, especially number 3 in the list below… So, oopsie! Forgive me!

Anyway, below are my top-10 pet-peeves—some things that glory-grabbers might say to steal your joy, just as something wonderful has come your way:

1. Well, I'm so glad to see that all my prayers for you finally have paid off.

Translation: *I have a closer relationship with God than you do, so you are blessed mostly because of me.*

2. That's fine and good for you, but don't you change and start to forget where you came from.

Translation: *Misery loves company. I feel stuck and stunted and I want you to feel that, too. So validate me, doggone-it!*

3. So far, so good. But have you considered ABC and LMNOP? And of course, there's the very important XYZ. You must consider all of these things!

Translation: *How dare you accomplish this on your own successfully without consulting dot-your-i, cross-your-t, know-it-all ME?*

4. You got those special gifts from me. When you were small, I contributed to your upbringing.

Translation: *I am the source of your power; all that is good in you comes from me. And I'll be darned if I'm going to sit back and let you or God take all the credit!*

5. Well of course you did that. It's a no-brainer. Isn't that what anybody else would have done in that same situation?

Translation: *You are not so brilliant after all, even though your shining glow right now is really hurting my envious eyes.*

6. Just be glad I helped you with XYZ um-teen years ago, or else where would you be today?

Translation: *If there is cash-money involved, I intend to get mine.*

7. Yes, yes. We all have been through something similar in life, and things just always have a way of working themselves out—for everybody.

Translation: *Been there; done that. Didn't do it quite so well... But you are not special! Now, let's talk about special-me.*

Perfecting the Dance

8. I'm not surprised. Isn't winning what you always do?

Translation: *I am not impressed. I am in control. I shall not be moved.*

9. I'm happy for you because it seems to be something that is important to you. It really wouldn't be quite so important to me.

Translation: *I don't take chances doing anything that I don't do well. I don't think I can do this well, so I refuse to think that it's important.*

10. Give God ALL the Glory!

Translation: *Don't you dare take an ounce of credit for doing something better than I might have done it. God, I'll allow for… but you—never!*

Okay, that's my list. I'm sure you can think of a few others. Meanwhile, watch out for those glory-grabbers! Don't let them steal your joy.

Lesson 6:
Digging for Dirt

Nosey folks seem to specialize in fixing their eyes on getting to the bottom of things.

They know that if you dig deeply enough into anything, eventually you are going to find some dirt at the bottom of it.

They know that anyone who appears to walk on water probably has some muddy footprints along that path.

But is the dirt that we unearth a statement of the other person's character? Is it a testimony of the other person's worth? Or is a statement of the lengths to which we are willing to go just to contribute toward somebody else being hurt?

One of the awesome things about humility is that it can teach us compassion. Nothing cures the inclination toward being critical, judgmental, insensitive or mud-slinging toward others than being humbled by the vulnerabilities that lie along our own path of truths.

So truly, in that regard, each of us needs to learn how to mind our own business—how to till our own soil. Roll-up our sleeves and dig ditches through our own piles of dirt.

Because there is where we can find our own opportunities for forgiveness from others who, along the way, we might've hurt.

Let's stop making mud-pies, and just make peace.

Lesson 7:
Permission Granted

Stop asking for other people's permission to pursue your dreams; to serve your purpose; to enjoy your blessings; to affirm your worth—to live your God-given life.

The ego of your personality may long to be fed with approvals. But the spirit of your soul simply longs to be re-awakened—to explore an epic story that unleashes all the love and glory churning around inside of you.

You are a powerful expression of the Universe.

In the moment that you were given birth, in each moment that you are given breath—you also are given the highest permission you'll ever need to live your fullest life.

·•❋✺❋•·

Lesson 8:
Affirmation: I am Enough

It is painful to feel you are being constantly judged by someone you look toward to feel loved. To feel that even when you give your very best, it still might be not quite good enough. To feel that you might lose love if you are not "the best" in the pack.

Judgment can make us feel that we are walking a tight-rope in the heart of someone we love. It provokes us to keep proving ourselves out of the fear that one day we might be deemed unworthy of love—rejected because we revealed our shortcomings.

And there is no point in pretending to be someone other than yourself to try to fill someone else's requirements. Pretense undermines your self-confidence because it is a way of saying to yourself that, in this situation or around this person, who I am is not good enough.

But here's the thing. Recognize that people who are inclined to critically judge the people that they love do so because there is something inside them that does not feel complete or good enough. There is some void in them that they are looking to their loved ones to constantly fill for them.

But voids in human hearts and ripples in the human spirit can only be filled and soothed by a perfect love. And only God's Love is perfect.

So let them look to God for the perfection they seek.

Respect may have its "conditions" but love rarely does. Merits, mistakes and mediocrity are not measures by which true love can be earned or withheld.

Love will never ask you to compete for it. It only will ask that you allow it to give itself to the love it sees in you.

And just generally speaking, whenever other human beings start offering their opinions of our worth, we really need to step back and ask ourselves: "What here are golden nuggets and what here are merely stones and rope?"

Golden nuggets intend to help us grow. Stones intend to cause us pain. And rope intends to manipulate us and "put us in our place."

Certainly we should never be so thin-skinned that we can't receive counsel unless it is gold-plated. But we also should never give anyone the permission and the power to reduce us to ashes at the mere stroke of an opinion.

You are always "enough." And with self-love as an alchemy, you can convert even ropes and stones into golden nuggets—insights that can help you to continue to grow and shine, even if only in terms of your wisdom in choosing those from whom you accept counsel. Living is about growing; growing requires nurturing; nurturing is steeped in love.

Perfecting the Dance

So where you feel there are opportunities for self-growth, seek the company and the counsel of solid-gold souls—those who will speak a loving truth to you; those who know and value your human worth; those who see you always as a golden child of God, worthy of golden nuggets.

AFFIRMATION:
Today I remember that I have the right to be imperfectly human. I have the right to be loved—even when I am not producing excellence, even when I am not operating at my best. I have the right to give love and feel loved by others simply for who I am—because I am solid-gold and I am absolutely enough.

Lesson 9:
Affirmation: I am a Resource

God, please make me less concerned with what other people say and do. And keep me ever mindful that the Source of my life is You.

Please steadily plant my weary feet that I might complete your highest course. And remind me daily that, through You, I channel an awesome force.

For we are merely resources.
And You, alone, are Source.

You are my Source...
for guidance, for increase, for Love, for peace.

Dr. Nesha Jenkins-Tate

And I am Your resource…
forever
for serving a Love that will never cease.

You are the heart of me.
And I am eternally
...thankful...

NOTES

NOTES

Chapter 2

Parenting

*The greatest gift
that we can give our children, indeed,
is teaching them to hear, to trust, and to heed
the loving sound of God's voice in their souls.*

Chapter 2
Parenting

Lesson 10:   Dwell on the Things They Do Well
Lesson 11:   Don't Create Holes in your Child's Heart
Lesson 12:   A Solid Foundation for Communication
Lesson 13:   Respecting the Power of Love
Lesson 14:   Children only Lie when the Truth Hurts
Lesson 15:   Seeing through Weeds & Planting Seeds
Lesson 16:   Tricycles
Lesson 17:   Let your Children See You Dancing
Lesson 18:   Meditation: Pray over your Nest

Perfecting the Dance

Lesson 10:
Dwell on the Things They Do Well

We must remind our children of who they are and whose they are. Where they are weak or have made mistakes is not the place where we should dwell. Instead, let's remind them of their strengths and gifts, and all the things they do so well.

Then, as they navigate their way into the world, their strengths will be their oars—for they will know they are chosen vessels with contributions they shouldn't ignore. And we help them to feel empowered when love and acceptance are in their core.

So let's make them consciously aware that they can equally and quite capably share the essence of themselves in a world that needs the wonderful gifts that only they can deliver so well.

·•❈❊❈•·

Lesson 11:
Don't Create Holes in your Child's Heart

I've learned five (5) lessons, as a parent, about recognizing some of the holes that can keep our children from feeling whole.

First, I've learned that we should never stand between our children and the love of the other parent in their life.

Never introduce barriers that block the flow of parental love circulating between them. Arrest human feelings of jealousy, bitterness, competitiveness or possessiveness and respect your child's right to build a loving bond with perhaps the only other person in the world, beside you, who is key to your child's sense-of-self.

And if you must stand between your child and that co-parent, let it be that you are standing between them from a magnetic place in your heart—pulling them closer together when they seem to be drifting apart.

Secondly, know that you inform your child now of how s/he should treat you later in life by their observations of how you treat your own parents.

Whether you treat your parents poorly or lovingly, you are creating a mental map for your own children. Their grandparents are elders in their "village." So heal the gaps in your own inner-child, perhaps left unfilled by your parents, so you can create a healthy roadmap for your children toward you.

Thirdly, never distance yourself from your children when everything inside them is crying out to you for support.

When they fail; when they make mistakes; when life throws a hard-ball that knocks them down; when someone has violated their spirit; when they lose self-confidence—step up and stand in the chasm.

Never withhold love as a form of disciplinary action—offering your love proportionate to how proud, good or bad they make you feel on any given day about being their parent.

Observe. Listen. Pray. Offer guidance and give direction so they learn a new way and an understanding that bad choices in life come with consequences. Cheer them on. Remind them of who they are and whose they are. Show them that they are still and will always be unconditionally loved. Feed their resilience.

Perfecting the Dance

Fourth, stand together as parents when you discipline your child. And also stand together as parents in your child's defense.

If you strongly discipline your children but then, when the time comes, you shrink away from defending them when they are offended or violated by others, they won't trust you as their loving protector. They might even view you as a bully—powerful in imposing your will on them but then cowardly in the face of your own equal adult-peers.

The easiest way to raise an angry child is to not speak up on her behalf when she is unable to defend herself. And an angry man carries a scared, scarred child inside for whom no one tried to free him from a victim's pain.

So we need to talk with our children, to speak where they cannot. Silence wounds the dove of innocence and love that they brought in their hearts from the heavens.

Yes, we should allow them to make and learn from their mistakes. And yes, we should teach our children how to fight their own battles. But if an adult violates your child, it is always your business, always—and never your child's business to face alone.

And then fifth and finally, give your children a foundation of Faith.

Even if your own faith is rocky, even if you choose not to believe there is a God, even if faith in a Supreme Being strikes you as so much fantasy—expose your children to the practice of faith. As they mature into adulthood, they can choose how and whether they will pursue a relationship with God. But give them the gift of that foundation. Otherwise, when they feel voids in the heart, they may rely on your love, self-love, material things, or other worldly influences. And are any of these really enough to sustain them in spirit over the storms that can visit the course of a lifetime?

They may stray away from the Faith of their upbringing, but it is a nucleus to which they can always return. So teach them how to go to God for guidance, as they live and as they learn. It is a reference from which they can begin their own soul-search should they ever need a spiritual direction in which to turn.

There will be times in their lives when you cannot, or perhaps even should not, be there in a hands-on way, especially as they grow into adulthood. But if you teach them that God is always near, and that they always have access to God through prayer, it will be even more empowering than if you could always be there.

Faith helps us fill our gaps.

Lesson 12:
A Solid Foundation for Communication

Through trial and error and some tweaking and refining along the way, I've learned these nine (9) lessons over the years, as a parent, about ways that we can interact more effectively with our children to create a pipeline for open communications:

1. **Start having conversations with your children early—** even before they speak. Sing to them, with them, about them. Engage them in dialogue about topics that interest them. When they struggle with verbalizing their feelings, affirm their feelings

verbally, so they feel understood: "You don't look like your usual happy self this morning. What's going on today?"

Too often, as parents, we wait until our children are teenagers before we want to hear what's going on in their adolescent minds, and in their lives when they are out of our reach. But by then, it's probably too late. By then, to them, it feels intrusive. Building relationships grounded in ongoing dialogue begin with engaging them when they are young.

If they are in the habit of sharing with you and trust that you will honor their feelings and not judge them harshly, it will feel more natural to them to open up about their concerns as they grow into adolescence and adulthood. As they face bigger life-challenges and make major decisions, they will know that they can confide in you.

2. **Teach them to respect others, yes, but also teach them to respect themselves and their own intuition about people**. If someone doesn't feel safe or sincere toward them in their gut, teach them how to honor those feelings. Teach them to move away from that person or those people and to share their feelings with you or another trusted adult if you are not there.

The earlier they learn to honor their gut instincts, the better served they will be as adults who are in touch with their own intuition. You can't be there at all times, so teach them to get centered and to honor that part of themselves that can be there for them, for life.

3. **Only share your fears when you can also share how you are able to overcome them**. And if you must share fear, try to share it with humor. Avoid making them afraid of things just because you are afraid of them. That is a disempowering

misuse of their imaginations. Avoid making them feel fretful on your behalf.

Our children, as young people, are not our caretakers. Yet, we can teach them to care about our well-being in ways that don't invoke guilt or fear. We can encourage them to do things such as these: creating art for us; preparing our favorite snack; honoring our feelings as we honor theirs; volunteering to be of service to others as part of a family gesture; enjoying the responsibility of caring for a pet; or any number of ways that teach them to share loving kindness beyond themselves in healthy ways.

4. **Don't push for perfection when what they really need to learn is the value of making progress**. For example, if they give it their best effort and are still learning how to properly dress their beds, don't go behind them and correct their work. That gesture is a harsh statement of disapproval and criticism. Be patient. Allow them to observe, learn and grow. Let them see you do it properly with your own bed and, over time, they will get better.

Meanwhile, smile, praise and appreciate the beauty in the slightly sloppy efforts they make to honor the home's decor. It's important that they take pride in embracing a new responsibility and that they recognize when they are making progress in their own development.

5. **Consider encouraging them to play at sports sometimes**. It doesn't matter if they are not athletically inclined; there is still much that they can learn about life and about themselves through sports, especially team-sports. But if this suggestion doesn't feel right for you or for your child, encourage the family to engage in physical activities as a form of group exercise, or maybe even just play games together as a family.

Perfecting the Dance

The reason for this is simple. Games and sports can offer them character-building insights and life-skills that they may not gain routinely in the classroom or even at home—things such as resilience; sportsmanship; spontaneity; showmanship; persistence; self-reliance; team-work; improvement through practice; playing one's role to achieve group goals; aspects of planning and strategy; and the randomness of chance.

Think about it. Even the card-collecting games such as Pokemon can teach them how to network and engage with others to expand their circle of acquaintances.

Playing an organized sport, however, has some other benefits, as well. It allows for another trusted person beside their parents to coach them toward influencing their performance. They can learn lessons about appropriate ways to challenge authority, adaptability to various styles of leadership, recognizing positive traits they may want to emulate when they lead, and managing relationships with people outside of their immediate circle of family and friends.

It can teach that they have within them the power to connect with, influence and uplift others, not only on the team but also in an audience of people they may not know.

And try really hard to remember that it's not about your child "winning" or "dominating" the game or the sport. It's not about your child fulfilling your dreams or competing with the accolades of your past. It's about your child learning all the great life-skills that sports can teach children toward building greater character. And it's about them feeling loved, encouraged and supported by you, whether they win or lose at any game.

And if your child naturally gravitates toward sports, showing an aptitude and a passion for the game, it is equally important to lend some balance and guidance there, as well.

The hype from sports-fans (young peers and even overly zealous adults) can be intoxicating to anyone, but especially to a child. So remember to anchor your child in a sense of self outside of that arena. Balance sports with other realities that teach an appreciation for family-life where all are equally valued and where routine chores and acts of service are equally important obligations.

Our children need to understand that life outside of their favorite sport is sometimes not as exciting, but it is important—that there is joy to be found supporting family members, encouraging friends, and contributing to the greater good, even in the absence of soaring adrenalin, raving fans, and the special recognitions that a sport sometimes can offer.

6. **Remind them that they are always unconditionally loved**. Long before they even learn the word, "love," children recognize the energy of love. And they instinctively gravitate toward it. Even before they learn a language, they recognize warm smiles, laughter, loving eye-contact, cuddling, tickling, playing—all as ways to validate them and make them feel secure and loved. So let them see your face light-up when you see them and it will remind them that they hold a special place in your heart.

Our children should never have the sense that our love for them is tied to their performance in any way. And they should never feel that they are in competition with siblings for a short supply of parental love.

Even when we must impose family discipline, it is good to remind them that we are doing it in a spirit of love, for their own growth, that they might learn lessons now that will serve them well throughout life.

7. **Help them find and recognize their special calling**. Look for the things they naturally gravitate toward and allow them to explore those areas as deeply as they care to go. Let them grow through structured guidance, as well as grow organically.

Your child is not your "mini-me," your "you-dot-two" or the "junior-you." Children are souls with their own divine missions. They are here to learn, to love, and to serve some purpose that is their own contribution to the world.

So help them explore who they are by exposing them to a variety of healthy growth experiences—art, music, dance, drama, public speaking, sports, debate, writing, designing, cooking, cleaning, building stuff, caring for pets, solving puzzles, travel, languages, leading, following, journaling, meditating, saving, starting an enterprise—the list of options goes on and on, as you well know.

Allow them to express themselves imaginatively and experientially so that they can know what awakens the magic in their own souls, so that they can hear the whisper of their own calling.

Then, most importantly, encourage them to share their new experiences and insights with you. Teach them to laugh at themselves when new activities challenge them to grow, or when a new experience simply turns out to be not such a great fit.

8. **Ask sometimes; don't tell**. While telling our children what to do and giving them general advice or directions can be instructional, sometimes we can learn so much more about our children, and they can learn so much more about themselves, by simply asking them questions.

While telling them what to do can help us to assess their inclinations toward obedience and personal integrity, asking questions allows us to assess how they approach decision-making. Asking them questions sometimes can teach them greater self-reliance and self-confidence about thinking for themselves. It also can teach us to do deeper listening when our children share.

Try asking them engaging questions that spark thoughts and conversation:

How was your day today? Which courses do you think are going to be your favorites this year? What do you think grandma would like for her birthday this year? What can we prepare together for dinner this evening? What options are you considering for addressing that situation? What time do you think is reasonable and respectable for you to be home from your date? What are your plans for earning spending money this summer? I've got this little dilemma at work and I'm thinking that I might approach it in one of two ways but I'd like some advice… what would you do if you were me?

And you don't have to always agree with their answers. But do hear them and, most importantly, try to understand and empathize with their thoughts and feelings. Make a mental note, too, of where there may be some gaps in their thinking or their exposure that still may need some family guidance or parental-filling—even if that doesn't need to happen until sometime later, beyond the particular conversation.

Perfecting the Dance

But never ridicule or admonish their thoughts, no matter how outlandish, and never totally dismiss their thinking. They are trying to be open with you, so don't risk slamming and locking the door.

Be open to learning something new, too. They need to know that what they think matters in the world.

At this point, I must share with you a funny little story about how this Q&A approach once backfired on me rather nicely.

When my son was very young, I made it a practice to limit the amount of television he watched and to occasionally watch his favorite TV shows with him, mostly to see how he was reacting to them, and to offer some additional context when I felt it appropriate.

Well once, when he was four-years-old and watching his favorite show "Power Rangers" I said to my son very nicely: "Why is Tommy always bossing around the other power rangers like that? Don't you think it would be fair if he would allow the other rangers to be in charge sometimes? They are good people, too."

At that point, my little boy turned to me with a blank stare and he said: "Mommy, Tommy bosses them around because he is the boss and the leader of the Power Rangers—just like I am the leader of my friends at school. And that is just how it is. So Mommy, maybe you should go upstairs and watch the TV in your room and I can stay downstairs and watch the TV in my room. And that way, you can talk. Okay?"

And then he smiled rather innocently (or perhaps it was mockingly) and turned toward the television to continue watching his favorite show.

Oh, well… Needless to say, I saw many gaps that needed "parental-filling" on that day.

9. Learn when to let go. No matter how adorable our children are to us when they are toddlers, our affections must evolve over time as our children grow in understanding.

Our ways of expressing love, our topics of conversation, the level of support we offer in helping them to resolve problems, and indeed our expectations—all have to mature at a pace that encourages them to grow into secure human beings and responsible world citizens.

Emotional maturity is not magically engaged by the passing of time. And adulthood is not a measure of numeric age. It is a measure of one's ability to make wise and timely decisions for which one is willing to be responsible. It is a level of maturity at which one can be fully entrusted with the hearts and lives and assets of others.

So don't expect adult behavior from young children and don't routinely accept childish behavior from adults.

If we fail to guide our children toward adulthood out of our own need to coddle cute memories of their childhood, or our own desire to feel needed as their superiors, we might do one of two things. We either might arrest their development, failing to raise responsible adults; or we might create a relationship in which they feel they must shrink and pretend to be small in our presence rather than be grown and honest in expressing who they are now.

We can love our children deeply across the decades. We can communicate and share mutual life experiences over time. But we have to give them the life-skills and space to grow, and we must learn when it is time to let them go—such that they can survive and thrive in our absence and remain in touch with us through an ever evolving love.

Lesson 13:
Respecting the Power of Love
(inspired by my Dad)

A child held in the arms of a patient man
who holds all the strength of his love in his hands

as he works with purpose and care
for the greater good and for the welfare
of his children

is a child who's been held by a powerful man
offering a role model s/he can understand and follow
when that young soul marches forward into tomorrow—

well-armed to disarm the world of hate,
well-armed with a sharp vision of how to create
a more peaceful and loving human state—
having learned to respect the power of Love.

Lesson 14:
Children only Lie when the Truth Hurts

Nothing breeds a liar like the basic human desire to survive.

When standing in the reality of one's own truth feels and sounds like inviting the wrath of lightning and thunder, a child may rely on fantasies and lies because those stories offer a disguise that literally keeps the human spirit from going under.

Abandonment, betrayal, rejection, neglect, violence, abuse: these can be overwhelming truths for a child to face alone. And having to face or hide any of these cardinal sins of the heart can turn any young heart into a block of cold stone.

But in order to disconnect from those truths, we also have to disconnect from our feelings. And a truth buried alive in its own dirt eventually is going to hurt. So as we grow into adults, the mere habit of numbing ourselves by telling lies can erode us from the inside, while also eroding the trust in our intimate relationships.

Our buried truths eventually implode, begging to be faced so that we can unload them in a healing place that allows us to work through anger and pain.

And when finally we move beyond our fear of "lightning and thunder" to reclaim some emotional honesty, we probably will wonder how we ever remained sane, hidden so masterfully under all the pain—because our truths are our roots, and soiled roots especially need the nourishment of warmth and rain.

So find someone you trust to help you face your buried truths. Those truths hold the power in the darkness. But you hold the power when you bring them into the Light.

And every uncovered truth gives you the opportunity and the right to move beyond lies and pain—to shake off old soil, grow some new roots, and start your God-given life all over again.

Lesson 15:
Seeing through Weeds & Planting Seeds
(a tribute to my Mom)

Even when my thoughts and feelings far out-paced my ability to place them into grammatically correct sentences of properly spelled words—my mom smiled and saw in her precocious child a sensitive poet, a writer. So she coaxed this shy soul to come forward and unfold by shining ahead of her a bright light. And she was right.

Even when my brother's stick-figured etchings of his favorite super heroes inspired him toward daring and mischievous adventures—my mom beamed warmly for she believed firmly that her son was a creative genius. And she was right.

Even when my brother's small voice could hardly fill the ears of all the members of our church but his young soul could capture and enrapture every heart—my Mom told the world that her baby boy was a great orator. And she was right.

Others may have bristled at the raw pride she took in her children, the way she draped us in her love even as she disciplined us toward good manners, responsible behavior, and academic excellence—but in my mother's eyes was a deep emotional pride oblivious to onlookers because she saw greatness in her children and she taught us to see it, too.

And for decades, as a tribute to her own greatness and in service to her own life's purpose, she extended that same love in the classroom to her thousands of students because she also counted them among her children.

I believe that our parents are, by divine design, the vessels who can best help us to deliver to this earth our highest purpose. What others cannot see about who we might be is very apparent to our parents. They can coax, guide and challenge us into becoming all that we are capable of being—all in the spirit of love.

A mom who sees greatness in her seeds can inspire their growth with just a proud smile or a gentle nudge—to affirm to their souls that they belong here with us, at this very time, in this very place, and that they are unconditionally loved.

So this is a birthday-tribute to my mom—as a testimonial on parenting and also to thank her for always seeing through the weeds to water the souls of her seeds—encouraging us to always proceed toward our own visions of greatness.

Lesson 16:
Tricycles

As each of us tries to tend to the old wounds of our own inner-child, we also need to be careful that we aren't creating wounds in our own children.

Truth is, most times, our parents tried to do the best that they could with what they knew—perhaps not fully understanding the influence they had over who we might grow into.

So if we are parents, guardians or mentors to young people, we owe it to them and to ourselves to try to become the best that we can be, that we might feel free to offer them our love unconditionally.

You see, the thing with wounds is that they actually will try to heal themselves. But sometimes our habit of re-visiting the painful but familiar places in ourselves only serves to re-open old wounds.

Yet if we must re-visit an old wound, let us visit it to see it as a sacred burial space, a marker for a moment that has passed on to a higher place, a reminder that we stand here now, still alive, having survived that moment.

And why? Because the Creator was always standing there nearby.

So there is no point in re-opening a grave. There will be nothing there saved but ugliness, regrets and pain. The moment has passed, leaving only traces of its love behind, that we might possibly find a new perspective on living.

Each generation is a new opportunity to break the family cycle of any hurtful, dysfunctional or self-defeating behaviors. Things your parents learned from their parents that they inadvertently imposed on you. Things you learned from your parents that you might impose on the young people you love.

It's like going through life pushing a big old tricycle. At some point, you have to stop, get onboard, and take control of the handle bar. We have to look ahead and try to rely on hope and forgiveness and faith, if we ever expect to go very far.

We have to trust that our old wounds are healing and that all the anxiousness we might still be feeling will eventually settle. We have to press strong feet to the pedals and forge our own new path toward perfecting how we love.

Lesson 17:
Let your Children See You Dancing

Let your children see you surrender to your soul—just having fun, being one with the music, feeling bold.

Let them delight even in seeing how awkwardly you dance, giving them a rare but liberating and memorable chance—to see you in joy, in the moment, in the spirit of play; honoring your own soulful innocence in the most carefree way.

And let them know that the body takes such wonderful delight when the Soul and its dearest old friend, the music, are invited to unite—to set aside the mind's worries, to see beyond the heart's strife.

And then your children's souls will delight in dance, too, reminded of those such magical moments spent dancing with you.

So dance with 'em
prance with 'em
and give 'em
the rhythm
of Life.

Lesson 18:
Meditation: Pray over your Nest

Pray over your children.

...even as they nestle in the womb... even when asleep in their room... even when they feel too grown to lay a head against your chest... even when they are out in the world building their own nests.

Pray over your children.

For if your nest has ever been blessed
with the presence of children,
then you also have been blessed
as an instrument of very special prayers—

Prayers that can guard, guide, and inspire;
prayers that can take them even higher;
prayers that can light a divine fire
to the dreams and the prayers

that are theirs.

So pray over your children.

NOTES

Chapter 3

Friendship

*A smile is a place of shared bliss—
where eyes meet and souls kiss.*

*If it is always all about "YOU"
then "you" is about all that you will always have.
But expand your view beyond you
and see all the greatness God can do
through you as a vessel of love
in other people's lives.*

*Each lifetime is brief.
Deep friendships are few.
Love and cherish the friends
who understand and cherish you.*

Chapter 3
Friendships

Lesson 19:   Friends Allow Us to Breathe
Lesson 20:   Love Needs Trust and Trust Needs Truth
Lesson 21:   Your Bliss is a Blessing Worth Sharing
Lesson 22:   Don't be Jealous, be Zealous
Lesson 23:   Watch your Watchers
Lesson 24:   Click "Aloof" and Poof—It's Canceled!
Lesson 25:   Life is a Drama
Lesson 26:   Standing in the Gap
Lesson 27:   Your Waters Washed my Wounds
Lesson 28:   Affirmation: I am a Witness

Lesson 19:
Friends Allow Us to Breathe

Our Creator earns our FAITH simply by offering us breath. BREATH: You don't have to figure it out; question it; judge it; beg for it; or see it to believe it. You can just relax, receive it for what it is—and breathe.

Our friends earn our TRUST simply by offering their truths. TRUTH: You don't have to figure it out; question it; judge it; beg for it; or see it to believe it. You can just relax, receive it for what it is—and breathe.

So truth is like a breath of fresh air that sustains the vitality of healthy relationships. If you can't share your truth, then you probably aren't sharing a friendship.

A friendship feels open. It feels right. It feels real. It allows us to laugh and cry; to make mistakes; to release and heal. It is a safe place where we can express whatever it is that we feel—and know that we will still be loved and cherished.

And if you are not living in your own truth, how can others trust you to honor theirs when it is shared? Self-righteousness, denial, phoniness, pretense, lies... These are all thin veils that can hardly disguise the proof that we are not living authentic lives centered in our own truth.

Yet, friends can help us to face our truths—so that our truths can be used as a sword to conquer our fears. And a good friend will hold your hand and instinctively understand when you are carrying a heavy load perhaps down a dreaded road that you, nonetheless, must travel.

A good friend can inhale your truth and feel refreshed by it, and then offer you the same refreshment—because truth allows trust to breathe.

Lesson 20:
Love Needs Trust and Trust Needs Truth

People have to trust you before they will share their truth with you. People have to love you to tell you a truth that they believe might keep you from hurting yourself—even when that truth might momentarily hurt your feelings.

But when people don't trust that you have the ability to love them in truth, at best, they will tell you only all the little things that they think you want to hear—when real Love aspires always to be clear; to do more than merely tickle the outer-lobe of the fickle ego's ear.

But Love dies among lies.

So while you may feel angered by the people who love you enough to dare tell you the truth, as they see it, there also may be people you love who feel angered by you. And they are hurting because they feel that they must lie or pretend in order to keep your love true; that they can't truthfully be themselves without risking losing you.

But Love can be firm while being affirming.

Love can speak a stark truth to spark a conversation between you and your inner-voice—for it believes in you and wants you to make a wise and loving choice.

Love looks deeply into your third-eye wherein lies the wisdom of your intuition. And it wants you to seek your highest path; to speak your dreams into fruition.

But Love takes courage.

And Love needs truth. And truth needs trust. And it is only through truth and trust that Love can clearly see us.

So open all your eyes and clearly recognize all the people who truly love you. You don't have to always agree but Love does need you to see and to honor each other's authenticity.

··✻✲✻··

Lesson 21:
Your Bliss is a Blessing Worth Sharing

There are friends who can laugh hard with you, and perhaps even harder at you—but who will struggle and strain as if it causes them pain just to simply smile warmly upon your good fortune.

Everyone likes to receive a good laugh: it feels good to have your soul tickled until it fills and then spills the raw juices of joy. But not everyone can smile upon a friend who is basking in a private moment of joy. Few hearts are big enough to offer more blessings to someone who is already in a state of bliss.

So what do we do with friends like this, those who seem unable to be genuinely happy for you unless they, too, can gain direct benefits?

Well, if they've been otherwise good friends, try being a very wise, good friend…

And love them harder.
And love them still.
And know that forgiveness is
in alignment with God's will.

You see, what they lack is not love toward you. What they lack is the faith that they have enough joy in store to share with a friend who appears to have more.

And what they've forgotten is this: that each of us has our own fleeting moments of bliss—when the heavens bow down just to plant a sweet kiss—as a message from high above, to lighten our hearts and remind us of just how much we've always been loved.

After all, our friends are our family, not because the same blood flows through our veins, but because the same love flows between our hearts. Our friends are the long lost family members we have found when we recognized parts of our soul in theirs.

So at the end of the day, let's love our friends anyway.

Why?

Because our capacity for love is limitless. And because each kiss of bliss is a jolt sent from above, not to magnify you, but to magnify love. And because love, like laughter, can replenish an old friend's soul with so much joy that we help them to again feel whole.

Lesson 22:
Don't be Jealous, be Zealous

God, in his genius, created no clones. So when we envy the gifts and blessings of others, we insult the Creator.

Have we not also been given gifts? Are we not equal in kind? Is our own light not equally worthy of the work it takes to make it shine?

Nothing can stifle growth and choke creativity like envy. And few things can make a person as ugly as we can become when carrying its aura.

When we feel envy toward someone who appears to be disproportionately blessed with things we wish we had, we may find ourselves thinking: "I cannot stand this person."

In that very moment, though, we must recognize that what we are really saying is this: "Why can't I stand in the fullness of who I am when in the presence of this person?"

When envy asserts itself as jealousy, it becomes very watchful, engaging us in ugly patterns of trying to prove ourselves worthy by comparing ourselves to others, or by putting other people down. It keeps us so focused on other people's gifts and blessings that we cannot see, appreciate, or share our own. It causes us to give away our own power to those who know already how to harness theirs.

But jealousy is merely an acknowledgment that we are not digging deeply enough inside ourselves to call forth all that we can be. It is a reminder that there is something more inside us that still is longing to be set free.

So don't be jealous; be zealous! Find the courage and faith to pursue all that you were built to do. Remind yourself that there's no one else who offers what is special in you.

Allow your own personal power to flow by cutting the vines of envy before they grow—for we honor the Creator when we stand in who we are and what we know.

Lesson 23:
Watch your Watchers

Sometimes friends and other adults may admire and "look up to you." Take that humbly and with some measure of responsibility.

Admiration and jealousy tend to enjoy each other's company. And a pedestal is a narrow place to walk and a high place from which to fall when others tire of seeing you as their hero, or as their porcelain doll.

And never over-share to the point of arousing jealousy in others, particularly your friends. Show some sensitivity about when enough is enough on the topic of "you." Over-sharing tempts friends either to avoid you or to vent to others about you. Perhaps it even tempts others to violate your trust, in an effort to knock your ego down a few pegs.

But never lose a friend because s/he did not keep your secret. If you couldn't bear the burden, why would you ask a friend to keep it?

Perfecting the Dance

So accept praise and admiration with an exchange of dignity by seeking and seeing what is good and admirable in others—holding that up as a mirror so that others might also see and admire themselves.

··✺✷✺··

Lesson 24:

Click "Aloof" and Poof—It's Canceled!

When confronted by unpleasant company or an encounter that seems designed to evoke a reaction, we all may occasionally feign indifference to guard our feelings so we don't appear vulnerable or feel manipulated.

Aloofness can be a familiar place we run toward in our heads to escape our hearts. And an occasional escape probably isn't so bad. Who hasn't feigned aloofness to mask embarrassment, at least once?

But when that blank stare gets to be our routine response; when we repress basic feelings like joy, gratitude, sadness, affection, empathy—to the point that others know our opinions but few know our feelings—then we've got a personal communication problem.

Even *detachment* requires that we first must care about something and acknowledge our feelings before rising above them to observe them.

Even *anger*, as ugly and messy as it can be, conveys to others: you have stepped on a sore spot in my heart.

Even *drama*, with its disruptive over-the-top-ness, can be engaging and heart-warming when it is sincere.

But cool-posing *aloofness* conveys a dismissive air: "I don't even care... You don't even matter... Why are you even here?"

Relationships and even casual interactions seek to be affirmed through an exchange of human warmth. So when someone opens the door to their heart for warmth, aloofness can only greet them with a cool draft, and it promotes distance and distrust.

We will never be able to express love and compassion toward others if we won't even allow ourselves to express our true feelings. And if we aren't honest about our own feelings, they can't serve us well in recognizing and honoring the feelings of others.

We retard our own growth when we don't allow life to grow us spontaneously in the presence of others—scared that we cannot handle our natural emotions; fearful that we will feel out of control.

When spontaneity and vulnerability become our personal enemies, we are well on our way to becoming robotic.

So if there is no one in your circle of friends with whom you can comfortably be your true self, maybe it's time to reassess your inner-circle and open it to people you can trust with your emotions.

Repressed emotions beg to be expressed outwardly so they can feel acknowledged. And over time, locked inside, they corrode our inner-parts.

Perfecting the Dance

So, say poof to that "aloof" thing!

Smile, share, shout, wink, nod, laugh, cry, pout... anything except temporarily checking-out of the human race with a blank face.

Aloofness locks others out and it locks you inside—buried alive and desperately gasping for a big breath of fresh air.

··❋❋❋··

Lesson 25:
Life is a Drama

Being asked to open your heart to honor the vented raw feelings of someone beside yourself—is that an invitation to "drama?" Or is it a plea to simply be a compassionate human being?

Respecting people who sometimes live their lives out-loud rather than tuck their ugly stuff away to swell and ooze and fester—is that courting drama? Or is it growing in character by building a tolerance for people who may process life differently than you do?

Sharing your pain with those you love and asking them to make adjustments so you won't be hurt again—is that invoking drama? Or is it speaking your truth to those you grant the power to live inside your heart?

"Drama" is feeling like you're training to become the new ringmaster for a circus featuring someone who seems to love to court disaster.

"Drama" is letting your heart overrule your head, despite every wise thing your gut might have said.

"Drama" is selling your soul down a path of descension, just to buy a penny's worth of somebody's attention.

And yet, any life that is fully-lived is going to encounter its share of drama.

Why?

Because we are only human beings and sometimes we use drama to try to manipulate destiny and negotiate karma.

Life is a drama. And sometimes our relationships will call us on stage to help the drama unfold—because drama has a way of shaking you out of your head and taking you into new depths of your soul.

Lesson 26:
Standing in the Gap

Sometimes God will move us to stand in the gap for someone else—to cry out for help, to persistently pray on behalf of someone else's blessing or healing.

Sometimes God will shake us out of that numb-state of thinking only about ourselves and place us in a circumstance where we must stand with someone else while He works on that person.

Perfecting the Dance

Essentially, God is saying that there is someone in need and He is moving you to intercede. He is prompting you to allow Him to shine His Light through you to help someone else to see the way out of darkness. He is asking you to stand on a mountain-side and be the guide to someone who has fallen into a dark valley.

But as we pray for others, it is not helpful to simply pray for miracles or instant relief on their behalf. And while it may feel expedient, it is not wise to simply pray for a change in the person's circumstances.

Circumstances can change but if the people remain the same, they will invite those same negative forces back into their lives again and again.

So instead, as we intercede through prayer, we must pray that the person is able to see himself or herself as only God sees. We must pray that they can see the truth as God sees the truth, not as life has led them to interpret it.

And we must pray that the person can be blessed with a knowing and a growing that is in alignment with God's will.

Because no matter how troubled and dark our lives become, if we can just open our eyes wide enough to see God still flowing inside of us, we can once again see hope—and with hope, once again, we can grab hold of God's hand.

Dr. Nesha Jenkins-Tate

Lesson 27:
Your Waters Washed my Wounds

All my life, it seems,
God has sent me the love of my dreams.
But each was a soldier with a wounded heart.
So He instructed me in doing my part
to help Him
try to love them
whole.

An old soul with a young heart, I really tried.
But sometimes even as I laughed, I cried,
as parts of me inside just ached and died—
while I loved with all that I knew how to give,
hoping the love we shared could forever live.

Yet, there was never a happily-ever-after tomorrow.
While I sought to bring joy, I only absorbed sorrow.

And then, you came.

You rippled across my path, all wise and bold—
with a brother in your heart
and a teacher in your soul.
And as I witness the depths of your beauty unfold

I can now recognize
through our Creator's eyes
that we were brought into each other's lives
because we share those soulful features
that make you my friend, my soul-mate, my brother
and, most importantly, my teacher—

Perfecting the Dance

To help Him heal the wounds that I sustained
as I nurtured the others through their pain
as He readies me now for love again.

So I no longer wonder how you see life as I do,
even without wearing my rose-colored glasses, too.

I just deeply thank you
for seeing through me
while seeing me through.

...and I have learned that we can love someone deeply, even without being in love. And that is one of the greatest lessons of the heart.

Lesson 28:
Affirmation: I am a Witness

As people reveal themselves to me, God, please also reveal me to myself.

Make me a mindful witness of my own heart, in the words and the spirit that I choose to impart.

And as loved ones open to me and make their truths known, please help me resist imposing judgments based on my own.

Instead let me readily see your wonder and your beauty, in the things that give them a sense of joy and pride and duty.

And then please make me not so self-absorbedly blind, that I miss seeing their need for love is as valid as mine.

Dr. Nesha Jenkins-Tate

For our relationship with others is that opportunity to see whether we are becoming the better person we so seek to be; whether we've learned to embody Your Love and share it consistently.

So God, I am a witness
and I am longing to see
that I am growing each day
into all that You'd have me be.

NOTES

NOTES

Chapter 4

Soul-Searching

*When the soul speaks to you
of its need to find fulfillment...
When the heart speaks to you
of its need to find love...
The first place to look is not toward others.
Look instead inside yourself and
toward the One above.*

*The dark times don't last and this, too, will pass.
So receive each lesson as a blessing
and keep on pressing.
God is showing you how to grow into your greatness.*

*I let the music fully occupy my body
until it leaves no space inside for fears and doubt.
And I surrender my soul completely to the moment
so it summons the dancer inside me to come out.
Then I dance like a sparkling prism—
totally freed for a moment from the prison
of my mind.*

Chapter 4
Soul-Searching

Lesson 29: Soulitude
Lesson 30: You are in the Making
Lesson 31: Trust your Intuition
Lesson 32: A Declaration of Interdependence
Lesson 33: Anger, Fear and Sadness
Lesson 34: How Wide is your "We?"
Lesson 35: Stick a Fork in It
Lesson 36: Shake Things Up!
Lesson 37: What's on the Spine of your Book of Life?
Lesson 38: Your Life is a Glorious Dance!
Lesson 39: Affirmation: I am Letting my Guard Down
Lesson 40: Affirmation: I am Opening Up

Lesson 29:
Soulitude

Be content as the divine instrument
who was sent to serve your Calling.

Consume what you need
in order to feed the center of your soul.

Absorb the things that flow and bring
you joy, wisdom, peace and poise.

And know that all the rest
is just noise.

Lesson 30:
You are in the Making

A girl is who her parents make her into.
A woman is who she makes of herself.
And a boy is who his parents make him into.
But a man is who he makes of himself.

You see,
our parents choose to give themselves
to each other and to give us life.
And our God chooses in each moment
to give us breath.

Dr. Nesha Jenkins-Tate

But we choose
how we will use those powerful gifts—
from the moment we make ourselves—
until death.

Lesson 31:
Trust your Intuition

When it comes to people, places and timing; when it comes to making decisions about your life—trust your intuition. Not your ego, not your pride, not your heart, nor even your vision, but your intuition.

Just get quietly centered, breathe deeply, and listen.

Your intuition is that inner-voice guiding you toward a wiser choice. It is that natural defense that some call our common-sense. It is that messenger who speaks from the center of your soul, a connection to boundless wisdom, both timeless and old. And the more you trust it, the sharper it gets.

Your intuition is your "gut." And your gut is your guide for seeing the Light of God's Grace constantly at your side. And even in the darkest hour, it still has that quiet power to be a shining face, beckoning you toward your highest place in a Higher Plan.

...because in the heart of your intuition is God's undying Love for you.

Lesson 32:
A Declaration of Interdependence

Are you strong and self-sufficient? Can you take care of yourself with no need to rely on others? Do you seldom allow yourself to appear vulnerable, out-of-control, or fully committed to anything that you have not had your hands in designing? Are you comfortable sharing your opinions but self-conscious about sharing your heart?

If you answered Yes to even one of these questions, consider yourself, for this moment, an "Independent Spirit."

And here's what I know about independent spirits. Sometimes independence is just loneliness dressed in full armor. Sometimes it is a crisp outfit worn by people who are crumpled inside, carrying unresolved issues about trust.

Not trusting that you can rely on other people. Not trusting that God will be there for you when others fail you. Trusting only that you will have a back-up plan, so that you can cover your own back.

Being independent almost always forces you to live among the characters and stories you carry around inside your head. Because living in your heart, living in your soul, living in your body even—causes the yearning for a connection with others.

We each have our own threshold for pain and sometimes life hurts so deeply we want to disconnect, so we won't feel the pain or be hurt again. But when we numb ourselves to pain, we also numb ourselves to joy.

When we stop feeling our own joy and pain, we lose the capacity to connect with what others feel, too. We lose our sensitivity, our sense of empathy, our antennas, our glue.

So whatever it is inside that you are afraid of feeling—that is the very thing asking you to give it healing.

And here's the thing. We can't walk around whatever lives inside. We can only carry it around. So at some point we have to face the thing in order to walk through it. For only when we can walk through it, can we leave it behind.

That might mean counseling, coaching, or intercessory prayer. But one thing is very clear: it will mean losing that independent spirit.

Once you start walking and talking through your fears and pain, you move closer to coming out on the other side—to arriving at a place that makes you beautifully vulnerable, easily penetrable, humanly strong, and fully alive!

Because independence, ironically, is not freedom. It is actually a prison of its own kind.

So talk it out. Pray it out. Cry it out. Get it out. Bare your soul to somebody who wants to help you let it out—because when you release what's inside, you also release yourself.

If you are an independent spirit, you are a human soul who probably has been living alone with fear. But the Soul needs to feel connected with other souls: that's actually why we are here.

We are inter-dependent beings. So let's break free from independence and fly with open arms into humanity—because that is exactly where our God wants each of us to be.

Lesson 33:
Anger, Fear and Sadness

Anger flows into the hands. Fear falls into the feet. But sadness settles into the Soul, where it can make us feel alone and incomplete.

When anger flows into the hands, it causes us to want to fight. We want to pick up a tool and strike out at something. We might even feel compelled to write or type something so we can pour our anger into words. Angry hands must be kept busy.

Yet, our hands can also channel that anger in positive ways. It can engage in healing activities—through creating or mending things; through loving touch and intimate caress. And hands can join themselves and other hands in links of love and prayers that can lay anger to rest.

Similarly, when fear falls into the feet, it causes us to want to take flight. We want to walk or run away; pace the floor; or advance quickly toward a safer place.

Yet, we can relieve fear by channeling our feet into positive movement—bike-riding, jogging, walking, marching, martial arts, dance and other rhythmic forms of grace—footwork that propels the heart out of a state of fear and into a higher space.

But when sadness seeps into the Soul, it can fill our every pore—turning off all the lights inside and padlocking every door.

And while sadness isolates itself, it still longs to be intuitively heard—without testimony or confession, without the utterance of even a word.

Then, longing for companionship, sadness can multiply itself in futile search of its own cure. But locked in the darkness of its own prison, only sorrow and weeping will endure.

Sometimes when sadness is too heavy, persistent or overwhelming, we may need to reach out for professional help, perhaps through clinical or pastoral assistance, to help us reconnect to the power-source that can turn on the lights again in our lives.

You see, sadness cannot see that what it needs actually lies outside of itself—for sadness needs the unifying power of Light.

Only Light can infuse the Soul with powerful jolts of hope, joy and laughter—throwing open our darkened shutters, bringing down sorrow's heaviest rafter.

And Light reminds us that we need to be in loving unity with others—for we are not complicated books sitting alone on our shelves; we are always a part of something so much bigger than ourselves.

And Light comes from Love.

Human communication is an exchange of energy—so our anger, fear or sadness is often tied to our human relationships with each other, the energy in the form of feelings and emotions that we exchange among, between and within ourselves.

Generally speaking, when human beings communicate with each other, we do so for two reasons—either toward creating bonds with each other or toward creating distances. And we do this either by channeling energy that is uplifting in the direction of Love, or energy that is conversely down-grading in the direction of fear.

Perfecting the Dance

However, it is important to remember, especially in human conflict, that the "person" is never the enemy. The enemy is the "energy." So we must focus on elevating the energy in any negative situation.

Love, kindness, respect, forgiveness, courage, anger, fear, hate, evil... These are nine rungs in the downward spiral of a hierarchy in the heart-space of human energy. And, as we interact with each other, we must constantly strive to reach for the Love. We must climb toward a higher place inside ourselves; we must reach out to touch a higher place inside others; and we must open our shared experience more widely to the Light.

We each have the power to alter the energy in any shared space. And while we can't always change other people, we almost always have the power to alter the energy that flows between us and others—and sometimes that shift in energy can inspire others to transform into a higher version of themselves.

But sometimes sadness causes the Soul to dwell in so much darkness that we are unable to receive enough light to see even the nine rungs in our own hearts.

Yet, the Soul is like the aperture of a camera; the more it re-opens itself, the more it allows light to enter—and the Light simply reminds us that Love alone, in the most universal and highest sense of that level of energy, can unite all the scattered parts of us, so that the Soul can feel whole enough to unite with other hearts among us.

Love—embracing it, giving it, receiving it—has the awesome power to free us from the prison that encases the soul of a sad heart. It opens us to God's Light, keeping us from the sadness of a darkness that would cause us to drift apart.

Lesson 34:
How Wide is your "We?"

Is it a *wee-we* that only includes a prideful "I" and a pitiful "me?" Is it a *weary-we* struggling to love and forgive all the holes in the whole of humanity?

Or is yours a *we-wider-than-the-eyes-alone-could-ever-see;* a "we" that lives your life large enough to set your big old spirit free?

Too often we can get trapped inside that narrow little world of "me." So every so often we need to ask ourselves: "How wide now is my 'we?'"

Then we must stretch ourselves into a "we" that is bigger than you, than them, than me… because the wider the "we," the more we can see that we were born into this life to learn to love expansively.

And Love is big.

As the highest level of sustainable energy in the human heart, Love expands us. It demands of us that we open wider. It offers us as blessings to the world. It helps us to connect and bond with others in beautiful positive ways.

Yet Love can feel like fear when we trap it inside. It can even turn into hate when it is too narrowly confined.

Perfecting the Dance

So let your *wee-we* go, and let your big-love flow—because the world needs you to help us all grow and shine.

··❋✺❋··

Lesson 35:
Stick a Fork in It

The negative energy that we often call, "the devil," is an undercurrent that runs counter to our purpose. It is a negative force that seeks to distract us from being our higher selves.

But think about it. When we are baking or cooking something, don't we sometimes stick a fork in it to test whether it is ready to serve?

Well, perhaps that symbolic "devil with a pitch-fork" is a tool for doing just that very thing to us. Perhaps, it is a force that comes into our lives to test whether we are, in fact, ready to serve.

If our Creator is omnipotent, and I do believe that He is, perhaps the Creator allows that energy to serve as a tool to prod us, to test us, and to point out to us those areas of our character that are not quite well-baked—areas we still need to heal in order to stand fully in our greatness.

When we encounter situations where hellish forces are being channeled through us or toward us, we need to take stock of the feelings that rise up as our impulse for response, especially those feelings we have vigorously sought to overcome—insecurity; fear; anger; vengeance; giving up; giving in; volunteering to be a victim; lashing out blindly; sedating; shrinking or sinking to a lower level of being; and so on.

So when we think of that energy we often call "the devil," let's think of it as a match-stick rubbed against our grain, igniting fire temporarily to spark a light from its flame. Let's think of it as a force that reveals those dark places that we still may need to heal or refine in order to be at our highest level of service.

With that perspective, we come to realize that we mustn't succumb to negativity. We mustn't allow negative energy to rob us of our legacy. We must stand tall in the positive energy that fuels our purpose and our greatness.

So ask the Creator for fortitude, a positive attitude, clarity and guidance—and you will be internally enlarged.

Rise to reclaim the bigger person that you are and walk toward your greatness—because God is still in charge.

Lesson 36:
Shake Things Up!

A *ritual* is a thing we do mindfully in a sacred space—because our rituals help us to get re-centered in our Grace.

But a *routine* is a mindless rhythm we endure in our lives, a thing we do because we've always done it. And a routine can become a *rut*, a prison of the mind by our own design. So sometimes we need to make a conscious effort to shake things up.

How? Here are some examples:

Re-arrange furniture. Swap rooms. Make a collage of favorite things. Create your own vision-board. Paint something. Build something. Cut your hair; wear it longer. Wear new colors. Try new foods. Try a new route home. Visit a place you've never seen. Start a class. Join a social group. Rally neighbors and host an event. Make a play-date with your favorite kids and play under their imaginary rules. Switch roles with your child: "You can be Dad/Mom today and I will be you." (Now, that's a big change and a revealing one, too!)

Here's a personal example. When my son was four-years-old, I took half the summer off and each day we moved his little Fisher-Price table and chairs to a new space in our house to have a lunch-date. I allowed him to pick the spaces and give them names. There was "Hallway Cafe" and "Sunny Day Cafe" and "Cafe Cappuccino" (a colorful vocabulary for a four-year-old)... It was change every day that was so much fun!

Here's the thing. Routines can age us pre-maturely and without the benefit of parallel wisdom. They can make our world feel small and bland, hopeless and loveless.

The Soul is bigger than time and space, so it enjoys our expansion. And ushering change into our lives can feel soulful and empowering because it keeps us constantly refreshed, opened to life, and flexible to change. And further, it builds fortitude for handling the changes in life that are going to come beyond our control.

So shake things up! It will remind you that you were meant to be a powerful agent of change in this world.

Dr. Nesha Jenkins-Tate

Lesson 37:
What's on the Spine of your Book of Life?

Time will never travel backward with us; it always will keep moving forward. So when we choose to venture backward in our Book of Life, we go alone. We may choose to forego the forward ride but Time will not be on our side.

If we insist on going back to read old chapters in our Book of Life, we may get stuck there, between the old pages that were left gummed together by the damp tears of our past years.

You may find yourself wandering through scenes set in old halls of laughter, but they no longer can lead you to what you may need to go after.

So don't keep flipping backward, not even to re-read the notes you may have written in the margins along the way. Just trust that the most meaningful notes also were etched into your soul where forever forward they are going to stay.

If we won't allow life to grow us forward, time will eventually need to throw us forward—because life cannot grow and last for a soul that dwells on the past.

So be fully engaged with each new scene. Look for the lines that reveal to you what your life will eventually mean. Absorb every word. Listen to the narration. Savor every pause. Celebrate each punctuation!

And as you encounter blank pages, co-author some new chapters across the face of Time—because only you can choose the title that eventually graces your book's spine.

Perfecting the Dance

This is your Book of Life. And while you may get many chapters, you only get one book. So expand your outlook. Live it... love it... enjoy it—cover to cover.

Life is yours to unfold and there is much to discover.

Lesson 38:
Your Life is a Glorious Dance!

In life...
You're probably going to take some missteps.
You're even going to make some mistakes.

Apologize for them. Learn from them.
Laugh about them.
But never dwell where you fell.

Take the next step and move on with your life.

There are no losers; only learners.
And with each lesson learned,
we gain new insights

about how to close our eyes
and how to improvise
and how to live our lives
as soulful dancers.

Lesson 39:
Affirmation: I am Letting my Guard Down

I am remembering moments when I felt I let God down:

Too shy to shine.
Too cool to act-a-fool.
Feared failure so I didn't step forward.

But today I can let my guard down
because I know now
that it takes courage to know peace.

··✻✺✻··

Lesson 40:
Affirmation: I am Opening Up

If we don't make time to nurture ourselves; if we don't foster loving relationships; if we aren't walking in our faith—left alone, we may allow life to wear us down.

We may wake-up one day feeling like ONE BIG KNOT... Not happy. Not feeling well. Not interested. Not interesting. Not feeling loved.

And yet, Love and joy are all around us, but our eyes may be too tightly shut to see.

It's hard for Love to reach us when everything about our aura is tense, tired, stressed-out, twisted into a knot, or tightly closed. Whether we realize it or not, the message we may be sending then is this: "Go away, Love. There is no place open here for you. I am closed."

So we need to check ourselves from time to time, scanning for areas that we have closed and making a conscious effort to open ourselves again.

We may need to re-open our hearts to laughter, to chance, to the prospect of romance. We may need to open our minds to seeing old things differently and new things in a familiar way. We may need to open our arms to embracing others and all that life can offer; open our mouths to speaking life into our dreams so that we can hear our own voices and believe in ourselves again; and open our lungs, breathing in life so deeply it cleanses us for a longer living.

Once we've also re-opened our eyes, perhaps then we will see all the awesome beauty and Love that surrounds us.

AFFIRMATION:
Today is my grand opening! I am untying knotted ribbons and ropes. I am opening new doors. I am re-opening areas of myself that I had closed-off. I am open to new experiences and new relationships; new ways of seeing others and new ways of presenting myself. I am open to the Love that surrounds me on every level. I am living life loved.

NOTES

PART TWO

Performing the Dance

*To love human beings
is to know what it means
to endure disappointments
that can disrupt a dancer's dreams.
And yet, and still, we dance!*

Chapter 5

Partnering

*In love, our purpose is not to "perfect" each other.
Our purpose is merely to "accept" each other.
When we feel loved and accepted for who we are,
we can feel inspired to ascend toward our own perfection.*

*To freely love
who you really love
is the heart's greatest desire.*

*Sometimes you just have to follow your heart
and leave all the "what-ifs"
in the capable hands of
Destiny.*

Chapter 5
Partnering

Lesson 41:   Let's Love Fearlessly
Lesson 42:   Awakened by the Music
Lesson 43:   A Sweetness that is Completeness
Lesson 44:   I want an Extraordinary Love
Lesson 45:   How Do You Recognize Love?
Lesson 46:   May We Dance?
Lesson 47:   Please Teach Me How to Twist
Lesson 48:   I am Listening to Your Heart
Lesson 49:   Finding that Missing Peace
Lesson 50:   Having Faith in Fate
Lesson 51:   Waiting to be Wooed by a Lion
Lesson 52:   Affirmation: I am on the Wings of Love

Lesson 41:
Let's Love Fearlessly

You touch me in the deepest spaces of my heart.
So it would probably tear my heart and soul apart
if our bond should ever end.
Yet life has taught me that I can mend.

So don't be afraid to keep me
and hold me warmly
and love me deeply.

My soulful partner,
my faithful friend,
a fearless love shall never end.

··❋❋❋··

Lesson 42:
Awakened by the Music

You awaken the orchestra in my soul.

But if I were just an instrument,
I'd be a Saxophone—
moving you inside
until you close your eyes and moan.

And you would press magical lips
gently but intensely against mine,
then pour into me your heart and soul
as your fingers tickled my spine.

And if I were just the music,
then I would certainly be Jazz—
improvisational and complicated at times.

But always soulful, sensuous and soothing
and often merging with
the melodies of your mind.

And our souls would remember
how we moved together across time
to the synchronous flow
of the same mellow groove.

Because the music from your soul
awakens my whole orchestra
and it causes every part of me to move.

Lesson 43:
A Sweetness that is Completeness

I want to be able to trust
that you won't abandon us
when the good times sometimes
get rocky and tough.

And I want to be able to know
that your brave heart can go
hand-in-hand with me when
head-to-head goes toe-to-toe.

Perfecting the Dance

So tell me, sweet-heart,
will your sweet-love start
to melt like sugar-cubes at the sight of rain?

Or will it grow wiser with the weather—
the hard-times bringing us closer together
in a love grown tall and strong like sugar-cane?

Because I want to kneel with you in the eye of every storm, and I want to know that God's Love still keeps us warm, until each storm passes and there is laughter again.

··❋✺❋··

Lesson 44:
I Want an Extraordinary Love

Beyond companionship…
Beyond friendship…
Beyond a relationship…
I desire a partnership.

And for that, I am willing to wait:

For a loving union with a soulful-mate,
working and building together to create
a legacy of goodwill and matrimony
that we can leave behind as a testimony
of the awesome power of love.

And perhaps God just smiles at my naïve audacity.
But I truly believe the Creator wants all that for me.
So I know that with time—love, too, will let it be.

··❋✺❋··

Lesson 45:
How Do You Recognize Love?

Sometimes it is not a matter of whether someone truly loves you, but it is a matter of how that love shows up in your life. It is a matter of whether your loved one expresses love in a way that allows you to feel valued.

A person can be in love with you but still be unable to show you love in a way that you can recognize it. And often times that disconnection simply comes down to this: a lack of shared values and a lack of communication to share those values—things that each of you needs to feel genuinely loved.

So, in love, assume nothing.

If s/he has known you long enough but still doesn't seem to know, then lovingly tell your partner how your heart recognizes love. Here are some examples:

I recognize love when I feel safe and protected. Or, I recognize love when I feel supported in my dreams. Or, I recognize love when I feel that you need me. I recognize love when I feel adored and pampered. I recognize love when you hold me closely. I recognize love when you listen and I feel understood. I recognize love in the way you smile with pride in your eyes when I enter a room. I recognize love when you are patient and loving toward the children. I recognize love when you surprise me with things you know that I like…

…or whatever is the love-thing that tugs hardest at your heart-strings.

Perfecting the Dance

And this isn't about a *right* answer. This isn't about some *romantic ideal*. This is about *truth*. Your truth: what love looks and feels like to you when seen through the eyes of your heart.

And once you've offered a framework of the feeling, kindly leave room to allow your partner to mold the love s/he wants to share into acts that speak to your heart. Allow that love to show up in a way that is mutually appealing and soulfully revealing for both of you.

And when it does show up, allow your heart to openly express its love and gratitude.

On the other hand, if you are just getting to know someone in the dating phase of your relationship, please don't show-up with a list of needs. Leave room for the relationship to grow and evolve organically.

Observe whether s/he even wants to know what pleases you. Observe how s/he interacts not only with you but with others. Strive equally to know the things that seem to please your partner.

Recognize the dynamics between the two of you, the chemistry of the coupling, and whether you naturally bring out the best in each other, or the worst. Notice whether you feel free to be true to who you are in each other's presence and whether you feel that is enough to sustain love in your relationship.

Share things you enjoy. Share dreams and goals. But showing up with a list of needs at the start of a new relationship can be a sure way of having someone either run for the hills or conform so tightly to your script that you may not know until much later the true person with whom you are dealing.

Love always leaves room for two people to communicate so that they can co-create just the love they need if they are meant to be as one.

·•❋❋❋•·

Lesson 46:
May We Dance?

Nothing can set the night on fire
like two souls igniting the heart's desire

for dance and romance, for fun and games,
for truth-bearing moments so raw and untamed
that they fuel the passions of an eternal flame
that dares to call itself by the unworldly name
of Love.

So let's take a chance
on that beautiful slow dance
that we call romance—

Because when Love is
the sultry singer,
even if the dance ends,
beautiful memories will linger.

And let's dance
so close
so slow
so long…

Perfecting the Dance

So that our Souls will then know
that we are
the
Song.

Lesson 47:
Please Teach Me How to Twist

God,

Thank You for preparing me
for the love You have prepared for me.

May we see each other through Your eyes.
May we rely on You to keep us wise.

And may we look to You
as we learn to navigate through
the many twists and turns of
love.

Lesson 48:
I am Listening to your Heart

I believe that when a man truly loves a woman—in a way that is precious and pure, with a love that, across time, can endure—she can hear God's voice in the way he speaks her name. She can feel God's warmth as he touches her with his hands and caresses her in the depths of his eyes.

So I have learned to listen to the heart beyond the romantic noise, as I listen closely for that human voice that is carefully wrapped in God's Love for me.

For that is a voice that can reveal itself as God's choice for me—the one I shall love passionately exclusively, for all of the days I have left in me.

So be still, my heart. And wait with me.
And let us agree to wait patiently
as we listen for the heart chosen especially
by God, for us, to love.

Lesson 49:
Finding that Missing Peace

No, my love, my feelings haven't changed.
You complete me. I complete you.
And my love remains faithful and true.

But I've come to understand
that you only know who I am
when I am deeply and completely loving you.

So now I want you to see
and to get to know me
when I am deeply loving me, too.

That's the only missing Peace
in our puzzle.

Lesson 50:
Having Faith in Fate

I love you.
And I know that I could fall
in love with you.

But we don't get to betray anyone's trust
or damage any hearts that already love us—
just because we feel wired to each other.

So if, in love, we are meant to be,
then let it unfold super-naturally.

For we are old souls visiting here again:
interwoven fibers of an ancient soul-twin.

And bad karma
is bad foundation
for good love to begin.

So I know deeply in my soul that our love must wait because
faith can only walk freely into the open arms of fate.

Lesson 51:
Waiting to be Wooed by a Lion

A woman who is secure in her love of God and self will be able to recognize a man who knows a lot about women but who knows very little about love.

So she doesn't pursue someone, hoping that he will change. She understands that she is entering a covenant with exactly what she sees. She knows that romance grounded in fantasy can take her to places where she doesn't want to be.

Romance sometimes can sweep us off our feet. But Love will never force itself upon you. And it will never manipulate you into a position of submission.

Love will climb mountains to find you. It will stand in the way of storms that might otherwise harm you. It will stand behind you, just in case you fall. But even with that and all—Love will appear in the window of your mind, at the doorway of your heart, just waiting for you to welcome it into your life.

Love invites you to come of your own free will—to join in the loving.

So ladies, it is better to be wooed as a woman by a man who has a lion's heart—than it is to chase someone down, catch him as your prey, and then realize that in order to keep him from getting away, you have to keep him trapped inside a cage every day.

A lion comes freely, fully recognizing his mate. And he wants you to come freely—trusting in him, in God, in fate.

Perfecting the Dance

So wait for that regal lion who recognizes in his heart that he must choose you—for he who understands Love will honor your heart as he woos you.

· ·❋☀❋· ·

NOTE: "Waiting to be Wooed by a Lion" was inspired by the sermon, "Protecting your Season of Change," delivered by Pastor Timothy Seay of Hyattsville MD, USA, on April 27, 2014.

Lesson 52:
Affirmation: I am on the Wings of Love

I deserve someone of good character—
who is protective, loving, honest,
respectful and faithful;
who loves God;
who loves me.

I deserve someone with whom I can
smile and laugh and love and learn
as we serve our highest purpose.

And so it shall be.

The spiritual partner of my destiny
will seek and see the best in me—
so I ask our God to invest in me
that I might offer the same love.

· ·❋☀❋· ·

NOTES

Chapter 6

Love-Lessons

*Choose me or lose me
but please don't confuse me
with someone who will wait for you forever.*

*I prayed to meet the love of my life
and instead I met God.
So now, the wait for a mortal true love
is really not so hard.
For now I know how it feels to be
unconditionally loved from the start.*

*Nobody is perfect—
and yet it still remains true
that there is someone
who is absolutely perfect for you.*

Chapter 6
Love-Lessons

Lesson 53:   How the Milk Man Saved Her Life
Lesson 54:   Observe what is Served before You
Lesson 55:   Sending Mixed Signals
Lesson 56:   What We Fear may be What We Attract
Lesson 57:   Her Story
Lesson 58:   His Story
Lesson 59:   Holding a Story Together
Lesson 60:   Mr. Asset, Meet Ms. Accessory!
Lesson 61:   Love's Trilogy through Pain
Lesson 62:   Too much Passion can be a Poison
Lesson 63:   When Opposites Attract
Lesson 64:   Time for the Changing of the Guard
Lesson 65:   Re-arranging the Rooms in Your Heart
Lesson 66:   Finders, Keepers, Rulers, Weepers
Lesson 67:   Center Yourself in Love
Lesson 68:   Wait for the One who Sees You
Lesson 69:   Surrender your Heart, Never your Soul
Lesson 70:   Affirmation: I am Growing in Love

Perfecting the Dance

Lesson 53:
How the Milk Man Saved Her Life

The hungry kiss he'd planted across her lips tasted like warm milk and honey. But as she waited for him and he never emerged, the kiss eventually curdled like the milk in a bottle discarded behind the crib of a restless sleeping child.

And the curdled kiss made her nauseous—so sick that she vomited and regurgitated every part of it from her every open pore—until he and his love were inside her no more.

And the warmth turned into a heat. And the heat burned slowly across her body like a relentless fever dragging itself across the hours of the longest night.

And when the fever finally broke, it left her trembling; it left her sweating. And it left her totally free.

And she realized then that the fever had saved her life, you see.

For it had saved her love for someone she didn't even know would come to be—offering her boldly only his Truth.

·•❄❅❄•·

Lesson 54:
Observe what is Served before You

Observe how a man respects and protects his mother—and know that he will treat you no better or, at best, the same.

For his heart cannot honor any woman who comes into his life—until he can honor the woman through whom his own life came.

Observe how a woman worships and serves her Creator; and whether she honors all doors of her body-temple with grace.

And be very concerned if the God that she now worships answers by a name that wears your temperament and your face.

…For when a man is reaching toward his higher side, he protects the woman he loves and stands by her side.

…And when a woman is reaching toward her highest Grace, her love can inspire a man to restore his faith.

So observe what's being served in the name of Love.

Lesson 55:
Sending Mixed Signals

Probably the worst kind of dishonesty in any relationship is emotional dishonesty.

Trying to love somebody that you can't even like… Trying to love anybody when you haven't learned to love yourself… Pretending to be in love with someone when you actually are not… Pretending that you do not love someone when, in truth, you do but you lack the courage to show it.

In almost every instance, these conflicting energies are driven by fear—fear of abandonment or betrayal, fear of not having enough; fear of rejection or loneliness, fear of not being enough. But without truth, trust and vulnerability, Love really has no place to grow.

Perfecting the Dance

When people are being emotionally dishonest, they act at cross-purposes and they emit vibes that are entangled by these mixed signals. The people who try to love them wind-up feeling confused about their intentions and about the stability of their love. And rightfully so.

Mixed-signals are at the root of most dysfunctional relationships. That toxic dance that can lead to a romance between love and hate, between persistence and distance—is not healthy for any relationship, whether romantic or platonic, and it will impact the mental-health and well-being of the people involved.

We were built to endure and enjoy the pull of other hearts tugging strongly at our heartstrings, but most of us cannot endure for very long the tug and tightness of a constant knot of uncertainty in our guts.

So we each have a responsibility to our heart to speak its truth, and to never ask the heart to wear a disguise. The heart was not built to be a place to camouflage feelings or to hatch convenient little lies.

So it is better to hurt someone momentarily with a gentle dose of the truth than to allow a person to jump through a-million-and-one hoops in pursuit of a heart that is only available to share something unloving or aloof.

And it is better to confess your love to someone even when you know those feelings will not be returned, rather than withhold the kind ways and words of Love because you are fearful of getting burned.

So let your truth be known, even if you may need to later retreat to replenish yourself for a new love that will come to you complete.

The heart can recover from any pain, and ultimately it is strength and wisdom that it gains, when it recognizes that its feelings have been expressed from a place that was centered in its own truthfulness.

Your heart is meant to be a sacred space, an expression of Grace, a healing place for Love. Keep it peaceful, truthful, passionate and pure.

Lesson 56:
What We Fear may be What We Attract

Sometimes it isn't commitment that we fear in our relationships. Instead, what we really fear is "The Bra"—Betrayal, Rejection, and Abandonment.

Fearing betrayal, we might ask: "How can I trust that s/he loves me for who I am and not what I have?" Then, we betray the trust of someone who loves us by having a fall-back plan or a second jar of honey on the shelf.

Fearing rejection, we might offer only "cool and aloof" when what we really feel is so much deeper than that. Or, we may act-out in a manner we know is unacceptable to a person who fell in love with the better human being s/he saw in us. And when that person rejects our behavior, we feel rejected.

Fearing abandonment, we might ask: "How do I know that s/he won't eventually leave me for someone richer, smarter, younger, better-looking…?" Then we break promises or fail to be supportive when needed, leaving the one we love feeling emotionally abandoned.

Love requires some vulnerability. And that can be hard. We may still feel bound by "The Bra" of our upbringing, or wounds from our past relationships may still be raw.

Therefore, before we embark on a new relationship, we owe it to ourselves to heal the hurt inside us that might cause us to hurt others who try to love us. Then, so that we aren't perpetuating bad patterns, we might want to observe more closely whether our love-interest is also on a healing path—and is ready to work together to build a healthy relationship.

So it's time to throw out all of the old BRA's and set your loving spirit free. Love hard. Love freely. Love healthily. And don't hurt people—because when we hurt the people who love us because we are fearful that they might hurt us, we actually wind up hurting ourselves even more.

Lesson 57:
Her Story

He tried his best to possess and impress her—with lots of gifts, worldly goods, and shiny stuff. But all she really wanted was his love, kindness, and understanding. For her, that was beautifully and totally enough.

And then, finally when he came to realize that, he also recognized that her love was too expensive for his heart.

And if she'd wanted his money, perhaps she'd still be his honey. But what she wanted was the depths of his heart.

So today, the two lovers stand very much apart.

·•❋✻❋•·

Lesson 58:
His Story

Her laughter always lingered to tickle his heart, even long after she was gone. But a darkness descended upon him once he noticed that the sparkle in her eyes had moved on.

He liked taking her places she'd never been; offering her the gifts of his affection; wanting her to know that she could always feel safe under his provision and protection.

But she reluctantly accepted his love-tokens—it seems, almost from the very start. And if she so readily could reject his material gifts, what might she do then with his heart?

And if he had to feel alone, couldn't he do that on his own?

So he stopped offering his time and his gifts; sometimes he'd even forget to call—because it's hard to penetrate a woman who hides behind a fortress wall.

·•❋✻❋•·

Perfecting the Dance

Lesson 59:
Holding a Story Together

If you only can see the love-story from your side,
the narrator is an isolated voice of foolish pride.

So talk it over with your lover—
and then perhaps you can discover

whether One Love
can help two hearts
to start anew.

But this time,
with the Divine
at the center, as the glue.

Lesson 60:
Mr. Asset, Meet Ms. Accessory!

Let's talk about the assets and accessories in our lives.

Accessories are things we wear to enhance our image. They bring us to other people's attention. They are non-essential items that are a signature of our personal style. We usually have many accessories from which to choose to satisfy our mood or the current trend.

Now consider this: Some men think of women as their *accessories*.

…Does Ms. Accessory make me look good? Do other men admire her and envy the fact that she belongs to me? Should I get a few others like her—in various shapes, shades and sizes and keep them in my drawers and in my closet?

Now, let's turn the page, and talk about our assets. Assets are often centered on material acquisitions. They increase our wealth because they grow in value over time. They even create opportunities for us to accrue more assets because they improve our net-worth. They can serve as collateral.

Now consider this: Some women think of men as their *assets*.

…Can Mr. Asset take care of me financially? Can he buy me nice things? Is his money funny, or is he financially stable? If I invest my time, will his interest in me increase over time? Will other optional assets now find me more interesting?

So, how is it that some men come to think of women as *accessories*? Maybe sometimes women themselves inadvertently contribute to that perception.

Think about it, ladies. If your whole presentation of yourself is tied to your appearance (what you wear, your shape, your size, your coloring) and not also tied to who you are inside as a human being—how easy would it be for a man to simply see you as an option among his accessories?

And here's the thing: Just because you get his attention doesn't mean you'll also get his love and affection.

Then on the flip side, why do some women see men as potential *assets*? Perhaps some men inadvertently contribute to that perception.

Perfecting the Dance

Think about it, gentlemen. If your whole presentation of yourself is tied to what you have (your money, your job, your car, your earning-power, your bling, etc.) and not also tied to who you are inside as a human being—how easy would it be for a woman to simply see you as an asset that she longs to possess?

And here's the thing: Just because she's impressed with you doesn't mean that she's in love with you.

Some people cannot look into another's heart and soul. They can only look at their hands or other body parts—because they are looking for someone to do something for them, to provide for them, to make them look and feel good about themselves.

But Love looks first and foremost into the loved one's face—wanting to see in that person's face that s/he is pleased with us and still finds us worthy of Love.

Our humanness is maybe less than 5 percent that which we present to the world and likely over 95 percent that which we carry inside—the stuff that shapes the mind, heart, soul and character; the stuff that flows across our face.

Once we realize that, we also realize that we can never feel valued by others until we value our whole soul, our true selves, our real-deal, by authentically integrating all of that into our presentation of ourselves.

Love is about intimacy. So please don't settle for being someone's asset or someone's accessory.

If you can't be completely human and deeply real, then it will be hard to attract a partner who truly honors all that you feel.

·•❋❋❋•·

Lesson 61:
Love's Trilogy through Pain

Hurt people
will hurt other people
because pain, fear and hate
are the feelings they associate
with Love.

Whole people
will hold other people
uplifted in prayer
until hurt people can
stop hurting others
by acting out of fear.

But prepare your core for nothing more
than some heart-break and some pain, for sure,
with one too many false starts—

until hurting people can give each other
the space and the grace to re-discover
the courage to heal their own hearts.

Lesson 62:
Too much Passion can be a Poison

So your last love bored you to pieces: too dull, too nice, too easy-going.... In fact, s/he had virtually no sex-appeal.

You sat around watching wet paint dry on the walls. And for excitement—you held hands while watching the paint peel.

Narrowly escaping a death by way of boredom, you set out to find passion; but unfortunately, it was on the heels of Karma.

So while your new love has all the passion that you had wished for—between you, there is always some kind of "drama."

In any relationship, there are at least three elements. There is you. There is me. And then there's our chemistry.

And sometimes the chemistry can be toxic—a thing that can vacillate on any given date between hot-love and cold-hate.

So in the end, you may discover
that what each of you has is not a lover
but an addiction—and it's to each other.

And ironically, you may need to admit
that the two of you together are a very bad fit.
And the only real cure may be to completely split.

Just quit.
That's it!
Cold turkey.

Lesson 63:
When Opposites Attract

Sometimes what attracts us to people is seeing in them what we need to reconcile and heal inside ourselves. We see traits that intrigue us because they feel so opposite that they make us feel complete.

We see someone who feels like a fit for the gap we haven't been able to fill inside our hearts.

And while the pull of perceived polar opposites may create a tension that leads to attraction, it takes a strong common bond of Love to hold opposing forces together.

And if the aim is to love forever, that bond is made stronger when reinforced by multiple layers of love—from friends, from family, from faith.

The eternal bonding of any union of two people is more than the coming together of two souls. It is the merger of two families, two histories, two homes, two circles of friends—all converging under one roof—seeking the grace and the blessings of One Love.

··❋✺❋··

Lesson 64:
Time for the Changing of the Guard

For years, I busied myself with the soul-work required to clean up the carnage that often comes with any divorce.

I tended to a victim inside whose heart felt betrayed by her best friend. I tended to a naïve woman-child who is a nurturer

Perfecting the Dance

by nature but who God had moved into a new season to teach her greater lessons that grew her soul, so that the healer inside her could now unfold.

I tended to a wounded friend inside who needed to forgive her very best friend—the protective, playful, loving dad of my son and stepsons; so that from my anger, he could then be free—to focus on himself and his sons and not wounded little-me.

But even with all that soul-work, it wasn't until today that I realized that there was this whole other person I had overlooked inside—the fighter who had refused to stick around to feel like a victim.

Well, today I finally saw her face—still proud, independent and watchful of her space. But when I looked deeply into her eyes, there was something else that I recognized—and it was guilt.

I saw a warrior who over the years had turned into a worrier, carrying the guilt of feeling that she hadn't fought hard enough, hadn't known back then to pray hard enough for the family she loved—instead abandoning her home when the going got tough because her pride and her trust had felt bruised and rebuffed.

I saw a tired girl who had carried the guilt of robbing her child, at 5 years old, of a home where he could see daily the two people he still loves most.

I saw that no matter how much love and laughter she had brought into their new life, including free space for him to share the same grace with his dad, she could not shake the sad feelings she sometimes had. For she felt she had robbed a giggling little boy of a warm special place that used to bring him joy—a cozy place where he sometimes crept, nestled between his parents as he peacefully slept.

So when I saw that tired friend for the first time today—I wept.

I wept because I realized that in all my years of growth and healing, I hadn't even noticed she was there, or what she was feeling—still carrying that weight, while standing on-guard as my protector.

So as I wept, I thanked her, and I told her that this was indeed a new day; and that everybody and everything had actually turned out okay. And I told her that she no longer needed to be my guard—because I had grown my love, my faith and my strength in God.

And then she wept and she smiled with me, as finally—I set her free!

Lesson 65:
Rearranging the Rooms in Your Heart

Love does not hurt. But the heart does hurt when we try to toss from it someone that we still love.

The irony is that often times it is not even necessary to remove people we love from our hearts. More often it is a matter of learning to love someone differently than we had originally envisioned.

The heart has many rooms. So when our hearts ache, it just may be that we are trying to smash a big fixture in our lives and sweep it away with a broom, when it simply needs to be moved gently into a different room.

Perfecting the Dance

And while there will be pain and strain as our relationships move themselves from one room inside the heart to another, it is important to recognize which room will benefit the relationship most in helping it to stay alive.

Some relationships may need to move from the dining room of your heart to the kitchen—because in the kitchen, you can add some new ingredients, making some adjustments to the fire, to allow the relationship to simmer before you summon the desire to serve it as something nurturing to both souls.

Sometimes a relationship will need to move from the bedroom in your heart to the living room—from a place of naked vulnerability and heated intimacy to a warm place of simple comfort and casual joy where an old lover can be just a good friend, rather than have a beautiful relationship just totally end.

A relationship may need to be ushered into the bathroom of your heart—where it can be cleansed and reviewed such that transgressions can be purged and forgiven and love can be renewed. And some will be totally revived. But a few actually might not survive.

Every relationship occasionally needs to move from the private rooms of the heart to its screened porch—a place still near and dear but a place also where the relationship can breathe in some fresh new air. You can relax there and grow, benefiting from observations that come as light from other people you know, those who love you and who want to see your relationship continue to grow.

So when people are important in your life and your feelings toward each other shift, think twice before you completely throw away a loving relationship.

The two of you may just need to re-evaluate your dynamics to create a new way of staying connected, a new place where you can start—by helping each other to rearrange rooms in the homes of both hearts.

There is room in your heart for every person you love. The key is to offer a key to the right room—and to honor new boundaries.

··❋❋❋··

Lesson 66:
Finders, Keepers, Rulers, Weepers

When you love somebody who feels unworthy of you and your love, quite often that person, in desperation, will become your "keeper."

S/he will master the art of keeping your heart as a mate by keeping your mind and your soul in a compromised state. As examples, below are six (6) kinds of "keepers":

1. Some keepers are convinced that they can only keep you in their lives if they can keep you feeling *insecure*.

They invite you to disclose your insecurities and then find ways to constantly remind you of them. Scared that they themselves are not enough, they conversely make you feel as though you are inadequate and therefore blessed to have been found and kept by them.

Sometimes they need to feel that they look better, live better, learned better, run faster, and can even jump higher—that they have accomplished all the big things that your little heart still can only desire—before then they can stand on that pedestal someplace higher to declare their undying love for you.

2. Some keepers are convinced they can only keep you if they keep you feeling *high*.

They look away or they enable your habit of numbing yourself—with food, drugs, alcohol, sex, shopping, or something else. But fully aware of your addiction, your keeper does not intervene or encourage you to seek help.

An addiction is a lack of boundaries coupled with a compulsion to fill our God-shaped holes with things of the world. And addiction breeds shame; and shame breeds secrets; and secrecy can feel like shared intimacy for two people in a dysfunctional bond.

3. Some keepers can only keep you if they keep you feeling *guilty*.

They constantly remind you of how important you are in their lives and suggest that their lives would completely fall apart should you ever leave. You are literally their reason for living—a heavy responsibility to place on any human being. So you stay because you feel guilty about acknowledging that you are not happy being the structural beam in their house of cards.

4. Some keepers can only keep you if they keep you feeling *needy*.

They do everything for you. You have little or no responsibility or visibility into the upkeep of your own life. They manage your funds; your fun; how you eat; whether you speak. They plan the details of shared events. They possibly even may manage your friendships. And it can all be done so lovingly, so protectively, that you fail to recognize that you are slowly losing your own capacity for being a self-sustaining human being.

5. Some keepers can only keep you if they keep you feeling *confused*.

These are the mix-masters who send you mixed-signals. From one day to the next, you're not quite sure whether they love you, like you, dislike you, or have forgotten you're alive. They are emotionally dishonest, inconsistent in their expression of affection.

When they love, they love warmly and attentively; yet they can just as easily turn cold, distant and aloof. That leaves you constantly seeking to earn their approval, as the evidence, as the proof, that you are indeed worthy of love.

6. Then finally, some keepers can only keep you if they keep you *hidden*.

The depths and beauty of your relationship are not only private, they are a well-kept secret. Behind closed doors, your lover is all yours. But publicly, you are seldom acknowledged in the shared company of friends and family. You've become your lover's lie, and thereby, in that darkness, you've also become blinded to recognizing some healthy basic truths.

So recognize the difference between being in love and being in the prison of someone who is manipulating your mind in order to stay in your heart.

And if you find you are involved with a "keeper," the first step is to accept that you have allowed yourself to be "kept."

The next step is to remind yourself of who you are and whose you are—by reconnecting with other people who care about

Perfecting the Dance

you; by reconnecting with your faith; and by reclaiming your dignity.

Then ultimately, the biggest step is to turn the tattered page. Own your freedom. Escape from the zoo-keeper's cage—because you don't need to be kept; you need to be loved.

Lesson 67:
Center Yourself in Love

Not everybody who is alone is lonely.
Not everybody who is involved is in love.
Not everyone who is longing for love is already done
with being prepared for a long and lasting one.

Yet when we keep God at the center of our being
it doesn't matter what or who we might be seeing.

We'll always know
to whom we can go
to seek the company
and the comfort of
Love.

Your God is your source.
Stay centered in that force.
And let your life run its own natural course.

Love always comes to love on time.

Lesson 68:
Wait for the One who Sees You

There is someone who will see your body and want to unfold it—merely to see your mind, with no need to remold it.

There is someone who will penetrate your mind and see your heart, and will know to hold it gently from the very start.

There is someone who will pierce your heart and see your soul, and recognize a soul-mate without ever being told.

You deserve someone who can see God's Light in you, someone who wants your joy to never cease.

And as you "see" each other, you will feel God's smiling presence, guiding you toward a love that offers peace.

Lesson 69:
Surrender your Heart, Never your Soul

And when in love you fall,
may your glad heart surrender all.

But please don't ever lose
that right to consciously choose
how your gifts will be used
to serve God's Call.

Lesson 70:
Affirmation: I am Growing in Love

To say that we love God while harboring a lack of tolerance toward any woman or any man: it's like being madly in love with someone whose kin or children we cannot stand.

The Creator flows through all of us in His garden of things that live. And He asks only that each of us learns how to love and forgive.

So between me and mine and toward all mankind—
today, I take a sacred vow that I might allow
the peace between me and all others to flow.

And now, this much too, I know:
I no longer merely can fall in love;
I also want to clearly stand tall in love
as I continually grow.

NOTES

Chapter 7

Setting Love Free

*Dead love dragged back
is coming back to kill your spirit.*

*Never settle for being a victim
when you can grow to be the master of a lesson.
Never settle for being a critic
when you have the opportunity to be a coach.
Make every heartache and each mistake
a great lesson and a teachable moment.*

*Never chase after anyone or anything
that God has sent away.
When minds close and hearts contract,
there is little you can do or say.
Just know that if it is meant to come back,
it will return in a better way.*

Chapter 7
Setting Love Free

Lesson 71:   Breathing in a New Life
Lesson 72:   Beyond the Bridges
Lesson 73:   Broken
Lesson 74:   Love Cannot be Convinced
Lesson 75:   Incompatible
Lesson 76:   Mine ALL Mine
Lesson 77:   Loving while Leaving
Lesson 78:   Slow-dancing with the Shadows
Lesson 79:   Abandoned Dreams and Broken Bonds
Lesson 80:   God, is that You Talking or Me?
Lesson 81:   Bridges, Boardwalks and Cliffs
Lesson 82:   Set Stuff Free!
Lesson 83:   Affirmation: I am Giving and Letting Go
Lesson 84:   Affirmation: I am Kissing the Sun
Lesson 85:   Affirmation: I am Whole

Lesson 71
Breathing in a New Life

God breathed new life into me today
and it set my spirit free.

And this freedom feels calm and joyful,
and it even looks good on me.

I am breathing it all in and when I exhale,
I'm going to set somebody free.

Lesson 72:
Beyond the Bridges

In hindsight, one day, you may find
that someone you loved came at the perfect time
to act as a bridge in your life:

To help you crossover some troubled
waters that could have drowned you.

To guide you toward the other side
where your truest love finally found you.

So when Love beckons you beyond the bridge and it whispers:
"…s/he is not the one; your best is yet to come…"

Keep on walking; come closer.

Dr. Nesha Jenkins-Tate

Lesson 73:
Broken

In the stark, dark and trembling wake
of loss, emptiness and heartbreak,
the very hardest thing to take
is sleeping alone.

In the darkest vastness of the night
when all the distractions have taken flight,
without even searching for it, you can find
an aching heart, a lonely soul, a racing mind
assaulting a broken body, left to fend on its own.

And sometimes you may find that you crave,
not to be rescued from yourself or even saved,
but just to be held in the warmth of another soul—
to help you to brave the barren cold,
to bridge you through the hollow night,
to fill the canyons and silence the echoes
that can offer your solitude no insight—

until the morning comes
when you can summon the sun
to give you the strength and the will
to rise again.

Perfecting the Dance

Lesson 74:
Love Cannot be Convinced

You can try harder. You can cry harder.
You can grovel. You can explain.
But let me just make this simple and plain:

When someone we love needs to leave,
we need to let them go.
Perhaps one day they'll want to return.
Perhaps, we'll never know.

But as you face an end, know this, my friend:

Dead love,
dragged back,
is coming back to kill your spirit.

So let it go.
And trust and know
that life goes on.

·· ❋ ❋ ❋ ··

Lesson 75:
Incompatible

I love you.

And I see and accept you
for the person you choose to be.

But your choices are not aligned
with the values that are instilled in me.

So while my heart will hold you dearly, forever,
my arms must choose to set you free.

·•❋❋❋•·

Lesson 76:
Mine ALL Mine

The bigger the ego, the bigger the hole is that we need to fill with stuff that feels like Love.

We may associate ego with self-confidence, but more often ego is self-absorption driven by a fear that we are damaged, incomplete or unlovable.

So when we meet someone we think can fill that hole in our lives, we label the person "Mine." But the problem is that over time, the fix wears off, leaving us searching for someone new or something more to plug the hole.

Feelings of incompleteness and the ego's obsessiveness can lead to possessiveness—a tendency to hold on to every thing, action or person who has ever entered our lives by way of our hearts. Every one of them is needed to plug the hole that's getting larger.

So we slap a "Me," "'My" or "Mine" label on our stuff and place them under a big sign in our hearts: "ALL MINE!"

And it's not just the love-stuff our ego holds in our hearts but the murky stuff, too: "My journey… my pain… my childhood… my children… my ex-lover… my former spouse... my friends… my family… my failures… my credentials... my scars... my needs… my property… my pet peeves..."

Perfecting the Dance

Oh my, my, my… it's me, me, me... and all of my old stuff, stuff, stuff!

But people we love are not perfectly shaped to plug the holes in our heart. And love is not a prison to hold souls captive—in a shared cell with all our other murky stuff.

Truth is, we try to contain things because we want to control things.

Truth is, we cling to the love-stuff to help us feel complete—and hold onto the murky stuff to justify feeling incomplete.

Truth is, the hole in our hearts was created when Ego became the new God in our lives.

But the heart was not meant to be a prison. So we need to learn to set stuff free. The Universe cannot circulate Love and Light through a cluttered heart.

Get rid of the "ALL MINE!" sign. And as you let stuff go, let the ego know that God is in charge of your heart again.

When God is in charge of our hearts, that greedy voice of the ego is silenced. And we feel so much better about ourselves because we can feel love. Our hearts are plugged-in. We find fulfillment in sharing our gifts and serving our purpose. Our love allows others to breathe.

Then, guess what can happen.

We can recognize when we have met an equally yoked partner. And we can enter a partnership feeling whole—no longer burdened by stuff; no longer looking for the fix.

And we can avoid partnership-ego, that total absorption in each other, by not only loving and serving each other but also allowing the union to be of service in channeling more love into the world.

Lesson 77:
Loving while Leaving

Even as the seasons change,
they don't and won't destroy the earth.

For each season has learned
that, with time, it must return
to that very place for its own re-birth.

So a lover of life must learn to love,
even as the season
says that now s/he must leave

because
how we love
even as we leave
is a measure of our own human worth.

Lesson 78:
Slow-dancing with the Shadows

When you left, you left a part of your soul here with me.

And if we are not meant to be, I need it to leave me alone. I need it to stop lingering in every door and in every pore of every room in this home—so that my mind, body, and soul can finally be set free.

And if we are meant to be, I need it to bring you back home to me. All of you this time—whole and intimate, open and free—offering to me unconditionally the pinnacle of your love.

Because I want you to know that now I know that I can be—whole and intimate, open and free—offering to you unconditionally the depth of my love.

And I don't want to watch our shadows anymore, slow-dancing in silence across this floor. I want us inside the shadows, holding each other close, giving each other more love than ever before.

· · ❋❋❋ · ·

Lesson 79:
Abandoned Dreams and Broken Bonds

There may come a time in the union of two soul-mates when they will have to withdraw their Souls to make each of them once again separately whole—even as they confess that they have no control over a love that will forever hold the other in their hearts.

Dr. Nesha Jenkins-Tate

There may come a time when you have to take back the parts of yourself you have allowed the world to define. And then all the things you've held inside and labeled "mine" must be shared with the world and released to the Divine.

These are moments of re-awakening.
These are steps toward finding your peace.
These are soulful moments of mourning,
the wake before the burial
of memories being released.

But eventually, the wake will become an awakening. And eventually, the darkness of the mourning will lift. For you will be awakened and renewed by an early morning, clearly viewed as a sacred gift.

Yet during those dark hours of the night and even in the early dawn, the moon can be a wise but solemn friend to lean upon. For the moon blows a sobering draft across the Soul—leaving you feeling tattered, scattered, naked and cold.

But as you are waking up
from an abandoned dream,
As you are breaking away
from a completed bond,
As you are allowing the love inside
to stay eternally alive—
even when the union of two souls has died…

Just breathe—
because the most soothing warmth of your healing
is in the joyful feeling
that comes with each new breath of life.

Perfecting the Dance

These are your breakthrough moments.
These are the deepest lessons of love.

These are the divine gifts from which you cannot hide, for they have come to guide your journey through the able hands of the One above.

Lesson 80:
God, is that You Talking or Me?

Sometimes when we long for love and intimacy with someone who is not in our lives in that way, we justify the intensity of our feelings by believing that God chose the person to be in our lives. We want to believe that the union is destiny's plan.

Even as the relationship flounders, we might pray to hold on to it, wanting to have faith in things unseen, because we need to validate our feelings, our longing, our dream.

But how do we know when the response to our prayers is actually God speaking and not just us talking to ourselves?

For a minute, let's suppose that it is true that this person is the heart that has been chosen especially for you—by destiny. Now let's suppose also that maybe this thing isn't destined to come into full fruition until 10 years from now.

What are you going to do in the meanwhile—stop loving and living your life? We can never get ahead of God's plans. So if you really believe in destiny, then you know this is out of your hands. Destiny is in charge. Not you.

Recognize, too, that even in intimate matters of the heart, free-will is granted by the Creator, still. So the Universe is not going to force a person's heart to commit to a relationship that defies the person's will.

To live inside a heart compelled by anything other than the warm and sweet surrender of Love is a cold and funky place to be. And that should be nobody's destiny.

So is it really God's voice that you're hearing?

Well… Does it cause you to worry? Does it occupy your mind to the point of obsession? Does it make you feel fearful and desperate? Are you encrypted in a script and a timeline that play out in your mind, but in real life, the co-star can't even find the time to read your script?

These kinds of thoughts are not "visions." These are "prisons." And a prison is designed to make you feel isolated, lonely, desperate and unworthy of the freedom to live your life.

So very likely, it is not God's voice you're hearing. It is yours.

Because when God speaks and we listen, we feel humbled, comforted, relieved, awakened, and released from the prisons of the mind. We find the courage to trust that all that is meant for us will eventually come with time.

So ignore those voices. Own and love your freedom. Live and love your life.

Lesson 81:
Bridges, Boardwalks and Cliffs

We should never burn our bridges
because on the road of life,
every bridge is a Godsend
and a divine transitional gift.

However, we do need to recognize
what was a bridge,
what was a boardwalk,
and what could have been a cliff...

Lesson 82:
Set Stuff Free!

Whether it is old feelings, thoughts or material things; or simply people who have moved on with their lives—we have to be mindful about hoarding stuff.

When we feel alone and afraid on some level, clutter can actually feel like the comforting warmth of old companions. During those times, orderliness, cleanliness and letting go can actually feel like emptiness, nakedness and loneliness. So perhaps hoarding, in part, is a habit of holding on to familiar things while hoping to fill some void in our lives.

But how are we going to feel and operate at our absolute best, if we are hauntingly surrounded by the chaos of clutter and mess? We must clear paths to invite the Universe to bring forth our success. And we must open our hearts to new loving experiences if we actually want to feel blessed.

Things held long after their time will only build a prison in the mind. So set stuff free!

·•❋❋❋•·

Lesson 83:
Affirmation: I am Giving and Letting Go

Imagine receiving a beautiful gift-box. Your heart races as you eagerly unwrap it. You open the box and carefully unfold the lovely tissue covering. You reach into the box to hold your wonderful gift.

But lo and behold—your gift in the box is still in firm grasp of the hands of the person who gave it to you!

Unsettling, right? Well that is how it feels whenever we give a gift to someone but then we refuse to move on.

What are some of the ways we hold on to a gift?

Perhaps we wait around for the perfect response of gratitude and acknowledgment. Or, we tell everyone how generous we have been. Or, we heavy-handedly instruct the receiver on the "appropriate" way to use the gift, despite not being asked. We periodically follow-up to make sure that the gift isn't just lying around somewhere and that only the receiver is using it. Or, we audaciously ask for a favor, believing that we are owed something for the gift.

Perfecting the Dance

But when we give someone something truly intended to be a gift, we have to learn to let it go. Whether we give the person a present, a talent, an insight, a compliment, a favor, a service, or advice—a gift is not a gift until the Giver lets it go.

If we find that it is difficult to give something and move on, perhaps it's time to examine our intentions. Is the gift actually an investment; a bribe; a subtle statement of superiority over the receiver; a test of the depth of another person's gratitude or love toward us?

Giving, first and foremost, begins with the joyful intention of sharing love, knowing the love we share can be replenished by the Great Giver of Life.

What goes around comes around, but we have to first let it go. So a joyful giver wraps every gift in love, knowing that nothing will be lost in the giving and more love will be gained from the joy.

AFFIRMATION:
Each day I am joyfully sharing my gifts. I wrap every gift in Love, knowing that I am growing from the joy of sharing. I give. I let go. I grow... because now I know that I am built to be the joyful giver of many gifts.

Dr. Nesha Jenkins-Tate

Lesson 84:
Affirmation: I am Kissing the Sun

Sometimes, when we can't see the forest but we only can see a tree, it is because we are holding on too tightly to a thing that needs to be set free.

If that tree that we are holding is one hollowed by anger, fear or pain, maybe only the forest can fill it with leaves and strengthen its roots again.

If we are holding on to a tree we love and we aren't allowing it to grow, maybe we are trying too hard to preserve the familiar love that we know. That's when Nature may send her gust of winds, forcing us to let go.

So today I let go of a tree.
And now what do I see?

I see a forest of trees
extending their branches toward me.

I see a ground, wet with tears,
feeding thirsty foliage and honey bees.

I see a sun up in the heavens
smiling brightly through the trees—

reminding me
that I am free.

So today I let go.
And I just let God be.

Lesson 85:
Affirmation: I am Whole

Sometimes hearts break. If we live our lives fully and open our hearts to love, which is its life-blood, at some points we are going to feel heart-broken.

So how do we begin to mend a broken heart?

We mourn what was torn. We learn as we turn. We breathe as we rest between each of life's tests. We share with those we trust. We remind ourselves that God's Love is unconditional toward us. We forgive and we ask for forgiveness. And thus, over time, and with the grace of extending ourselves the patience to honor our own pace, we come to accept a new reality as we shift our souls into a new space.

And then, slowly, we heal—so our hearts can continue to love and live and laugh and deeply feel.

And this I also know now to be true: blue hearts, once healed, shine even more brightly—because they have a testimony of how God's amazing Grace helped to pull them through.

AFFIRMATION:
Today I claim a spirit of growth and healing for I have withstood the tests of time and endured some of the storms of life. And I know now that I was borne by love and born to love. I know that I am loved, in each breath, by my Creator and even by some of His loving creations.

I am a brilliant and resilient child of God. And today I know deeply in my heart that my love is growing bigger and wiser, and wonderfully whole. I am embracing a renewed peace in my soul.

NOTES

Chapter 8

Forgiveness

*Not fearing failure is freedom.
Treating people fairly is freedom.
Faith despite what you've faced is freedom.
Forgiveness is freedom.
So each day we must find a way
to set ourselves free.*

*Something lifts and shifts inside our hearts
in the moment that we realize
that somebody loved us as best s/he could
with what s/he carried inside.*

Chapter 8
Forgiveness

Lesson 86:   My Tears are Prayers
Lesson 87:   Forgive until You Forget
Lesson 88:   Blocking Arteries
Lesson 89:   Who do You Trust?
Lesson 90:   Feeding a Grudge, Starving your Soul
Lesson 91:   Lifting the Veil
Lesson 92:   Dance Lessons
Lesson 93:   When Bullies Grow Up: Recovery Steps
Lesson 94:   Thief in the Night
Lesson 95:   Forget to Forgive but Remember to Live
Lesson 96:   Meditation: Thanks for Forgiveness
Lesson 97:   Meditation: Prayer for a New Day
Lesson 98:   Affirmation: I am Built for Love

Perfecting the Dance

Lesson 86:
My Tears are Prayers

My tears are my cleansing prayers.
They flow beyond my face
into a healing place
of comfort inside God's Heart.

We love. We need.
We hurt. We bleed.
And, why?

Because we are human beings until we die.
And because it is healing for us to cry.

··❄✺❄··

Lesson 87:
Forgive until You Forget

When people we love disappoint us and break our hearts, so seldom are they doing what they actually meant. Not to hurt "us" but to relieve some unresolved hurt in themselves—was more likely their original intent.

But whether we walk away or stay, we must work through the pain in our hearts each day with a new mind-set: If it's still painful to remember, we must forgive and forgive until the pain dissolves and it frees us to forget.

Leaving behind those painful memories helps to lighten the load as you travel that bumpy road to reclaim your happily-ever-after. So try to picture moments clearly when you held each other dearly—wrapped in nothing else but merely innocence, love, smiles and laughter.

Lesson 88:
Blocking Arteries

When a giver stops giving Love, withdrawing it or holding it back in some part—it's as if the flow of Love were being blocked in an artery of God's own heart.

So refill your loving hands by keeping
them gently pressed against God's face.

And forgive those who know no better than
to take Love without an offering of grace.

For it is time now to give again.
So forgive now... and live again.

Lesson 89:
Who do You Trust?

The greatest casualty in a betrayal is the trust that we lose in our own selves.

When friends betray a trust, you eventually may forgive them. And that is huge! But do you forgive the person you carry with

Perfecting the Dance

you throughout your life into every situation going forward? Do you forgive yourself?

When we open our lives to someone who violates our trust—at some level of our core, we may lose trust in ourselves. It can feel like self-betrayal. And until we forgive ourselves, we may constantly second-guess our instincts for making wise choices in our relationships.

But here's the thing. Love cannot thrive in any relationship in the absence of trust. And that includes our relationship with our own selves. So it is difficult for me to love me if I no longer can trust me.

How does a lack of self-trust show up? We may starve our closest relationships by keeping people at a distance. We avoid sharing our deepest truths to prevent our story from being repeated. We may mask our feelings hoping they won't be recognized.

But in healthy human relationships, these "barriers" are never the answer. A barrier is a tall wall erected by fear—while fellowship, friendship, kinship, partnership, all require a willingness to break down our walls to share. They require some level of trust.

So the answer perhaps, for us, is "boundaries." Boundaries are the delicate lines drawn by self-respect. Our boundaries firmly say: "Okay, that is enough!" And they keep us from inappropriately giving away stuff—our intimacy, our history, our dignity, our sanity, and our or anybody's privacy.

Boundaries protect us from idleness, greediness and neediness—culprits that most often cause us to violate a trust, even our own.

Everyone you meet cannot be allowed in the theatre of your life. And everyone in the theatre is not worthy of a front-row seat... a role in the cast... a backstage pass.

God has entrusted us with a powerful love that is real—a love strong enough to heal anything that we can feel. So when you trust in your Creator and you trust yourself, you have all that you'll ever need to overcome any heartache caused by anyone's misdeed. Please trust in that.

Lesson 90:
Feeding a Grudge, Starving Your Soul

Sometimes there is a very convenient reason why people don't forgive. And that reason is that once we forgive, we are then left feeling fully responsible for how we choose to live.

When you feel you have something or someone to blame for why you feel disempowered, cynical, self-righteous or bruised, you actually can feel that you have nothing much to lose—because you are not tapping into and owning all of your greatness.

So some of us will starve our souls while nursing a grudge for days, for weeks, for months, perhaps generationally, for years—believing that the only way we can be spurred into action is through the anger that arises from individual or collective fears.

And when the only thing keeping us from feeling that cold emptiness inside is the smoldering heat of hate—we will eat hungrily when thoughts of vengeance or victimhood are heaped upon our plate.

Perfecting the Dance

But there is no freedom to be found while holding on tightly to a grudge—for the greatest way to feel empowered always is to remember that you are loved.

So when we learn how to forgive, we grant ourselves permission again to fully live—with open heart, wider eyes, bigger ears; and feet that are moving toward answered prayers.

The Soul's path for this earth-walk is already paved; but it requires a heart that is forgiving, forgiven, loving and brave.

And if the truth be told, that is the best way to re-open ourselves to allow God to feed our souls.

··✻✼✻··

Lesson 91:
Lifting the Veil

Some of us believe that we have a problem with forgetting and forgiving, when perhaps what we really have is a fear of fully living.

We may nurse old wounds because they offer us an excuse for holding back Love. We may inflict on others our harsh words, our distance, our sarcasm, criticism and blame—as we wear without shame an old wound as a badge of pride, a mask, a veil behind which we can hide, as we declare the victory of being the victim inside.

But just maybe…

It is time to lift that veil
and look down your own trail

Dr. Nesha Jenkins-Tate

and start to make amends
with the foes who would be friends
and look into your own naked face
and own all of your own awesome grace
and offer your brightest light as an apology
and finally know then that you are

FREE!

· • ❋ ❊ ❋ • ·

Lesson 92:
Dance Lessons

First, I learned to love myself.
Then as I recognized parts of myself in others,
I danced toward them and learned to love them, too.

Then as I grew, I learned to love God.
And right about then,
the dance-steps started to get a little bit hard—
because I learned that God loves and lives
in every living, dancing, breathing thing.

So I tried to extend myself toward everyone I knew
but sometimes that only left me
feeling drained and blue—
because all of me and all of them
were only human, too.

And to love human beings
is to know what it means

Perfecting the Dance

to endure disappointments
that can disrupt a dancer's dreams.

And yet, and still, we dance!

· · ❋❋❋ · ·

Lesson 93:
When Bullies Grow Up: Recovery Steps

It's easy to recognize a bully on the playground in grade-school. S/he's the kid on the prowl just looking for a place to direct a lot of anger or bad manners brought to school from home.

It's easy to know the neighborhood bullies. They are the tortured souls who'd rather act-out and terrorize the streets than face the anger, neglect or shame that awaits them at home.

But things can get a little fuzzy when bullies grow up. Without self-sought healing, the bully and the game get more sophisticated and toxic.

Adult bullies can transform themselves into many characters—but the most common, I believe, are the four C's—the clever Comedian, the critical Communicator, the manipulative Charmer, and the upstanding Citizen. Let's take a look at each.

The bully "Comedian" can be absolutely hilarious! They make your side ache, your nose run, your head pound—in round after round of raucous laughter. But s/he also has an arsenal of humor that is so subtly mean-spirited that even while parts of you are laughing out loud, other parts of you cringe from being singed; from being assaulted, not exalted, at the core of your soul.

Then there is the bully who is the critical "Communicator." Their playground is your mind. Volume is used to drown out weaker voices. Insults are precise darts casually used to poke holes into hearts. Sarcasm can be sprinkled so subtly it serves as a form of water torcher. And they must have the last word. Even their silence and their absence can make loud statements of disapproval and emotional distance. And these are done all quite sociably, cordially and dysfunctionally.

There is also the bully grown to be quite the "Charmer." Popular for niceties and perfect timing, s/he's the manipulator. Charmers pretend to be nice or needy to gain favor by playing on the vulnerability, kindness or guilt of others.

They intend for others to feel wrong or bad for not being spun into their web of charms: "If I act nice, you should do this for me, or I will not act nice." They control by withholding or doling out attention selectively. And that charm can quickly slide by the wayside once the favor is granted or if the favor is denied.

But the most complicated adult bully is the upstanding "Citizen." This is the self-absorbed narcissist who wreaks havoc on loved ones behind closed doors.

The Citizen demands levels of perfection that can be unattainable or unsustainable. Achievements will be flaunted while imperfections will be thrown into a basement trunk with all the other secrets and funky-junk.

So the empathetic souls who love a Citizen often feel as though they don't quite measure up. They may even feel pitted against

Perfecting the Dance

each other as they compete for what little love is there to share beyond what the narcissist needs to constantly feed himself.

Those who love a citizen-bully walk a tightrope. You must shine like a useful asset—but then you mustn't really pose a threat. You must gently but gingerly tiptoe—as you walk along the edges of a fragile ego.

So the people who love a Citizen seldom feel affirmed or loved unconditionally—for Citizens are in emotional denial, numbly driven by the need to have others feed that upstanding image that allows the bully inside to never again have to hide or feel ashamed and rejected.

The irony of the Citizen-bully is that s/he is best at creating a breeding ground for all the other bullies—victims who hone their survival skills while jockeying for love and acceptance under the Citizen's reign—becoming the Comedians, Communicators, Charmers, or the achievers who aspire also to be upstanding Citizens.

The other irony is that these victims may go on to attract intimate relationships with people who have similar traits as the narcissistic bully. The new relationships feel so familiar while representing a fresh opportunity to finally win the approval and unconditional love for which they still long. And of course, once again, that will not happen because narcissists are limited in their capacity to love without an Agenda of Self.

Ultimately though, whether an adult bully is the Comedian, Communicator, Charmer, Citizen, or some other caricature— you must make it understood that you will not allow yourself to be continually compromised into victimhood.

So here are six (6) steps that you can take:

1. Call it what it is.
Be very clear that you are dealing with bullying behavior. You are probably also dealing with cowardliness—someone who is trying to prove himself or herself worthy by making others feel unworthy; who believes that s/he can only feel elevated by diminishing other people or their accomplishments; whose sole source of power is the life s/he can suck out of other people's souls.

2. Show no fear.
Bullies feed on fear. A response from you that lacks fear will make them feel rattled, even fearful. So try to come from a bigger loving place inside. Short of that, try to come from a respectful place. And short of that, try never to "express" your anger—but do "confess" your anger while inviting the bully to show-up in your life in a healthy way.

3. Define your lines.
Don't build barriers but do set boundaries. Be very clear about what you are willing to do and what you are not willing to do—and follow through. And if you are willing to do nothing, say that. Be very clear about what you will not accept. Act on terms of your own free will. And harbor no guilt.

4. Let the bully sit in his own bully-s____.
And let the bully smell it. How? When they are acting out, hold up a mirror to allow bullies to see themselves through your eyes.

You might convey to the Comedian: "Right now, I don't find your words very funny. I find them to be abrasive and mean-spirited toward me (or someone else) and I want you to stop it now."

Perfecting the Dance

To the Communicator: "I hear what you are saying. I also have something I'd like to say, so please allow me to share it." And be willing to walk away.

To the Charmer: "I recognize that you want something from me. Please tell me exactly what you want and if I can, I will help you. But if I can't, I need you to respect that nothing you do is going to make me give in to you."

To the Citizen: "I cannot be a trophy. I can (only) be human. So please try to know, accept and love me for who I am so I can feel comfortable being who I am in your presence."

5. Know what you cannot change.
You can't control other people. You can only control how you allow others to continually show up in your life. A bully must want to change. So don't make excuses for them. Don't second-guess or repress your own feelings when you or others feel uncomfortable in their presence. And don't get dragged into their self-serving drama.

If you need to create some distance to nurture your soul—do that for yourself. Yet try to look for the best in others—even the bully who is striving to change. Allow others to see and be the best in themselves without feeling compelled to remind them of the hurtful being they may have once been.

6. See your own inner-C's.
You might have some stuff of your own that you need to unpack to avoid having a negative impact on the people you love. So recognize your own inner-C's—your comedian, communicator, charmer, citizen—and give them permission to leave. Ask the ugly behavior and the bad feelings to stop showing up in your life, and apologize to those who they have harmed.

Be willing to say: "Uh-oh, I'm doing my C-thing again. But I am big enough now to be doing my God-thing!"

And as the C's leave, you might feel the need to fill some old familiar places that are now just empty spaces, so seek help and guidance in refilling yourself—with faith and more faith, with hope and more hope, with Love and more good Love.

Lesson 94:
Thief in the Night

Forgiveness is a masterful thief.

It can rob you of everything you own:
your excuses, your crutches,
your anger, your grief…

It can tear down walls and leave you naked,
begging God to cover you in a bigger belief.

And in the absence of any healing apologies,
and when the pain and blame
are still all that one sees—

It might even feel easier to wrestle the thief—rather than letting Forgiveness steal your worries and grief, to finally offer you the comfort of loving relief.

Lesson 95:
Forget to Forgive but Remember to Live

Sometimes when we feel betrayed by love, we have to forget in order to forgive.

And in that process of forgetting, we may feel that not only must we forget the bad things but the good things, too, because while we are still seeing ourselves through a victim's eyes, even the good things feel like they were merely a disguise designed to blind us to all the things that were untrue.

Yet, there will come a time when Love will come back to find us because it simply then wants to remind us that while the relationship may not have been perfect, there were some treasurable moments when the love was very real.

It might come when you happen upon an old photograph; a forgotten gift; an old song; a special place; or seeing your shared love carved so beautifully into the lines of your child's face; or perhaps just a random memory so powerful that it allows you to feel a joy so palpable that it refuses to remain concealed.

So we rob ourselves when we throw away everything in order to start anew, even as we recognize that sometimes, temporarily, that is exactly what we have to do—before we can begin our journey toward healing.

But once we have forgiven and we've cleared the slate, we owe it to ourselves to re-visit our fate to collect all the beautiful gifts it once offered us in the spirit of love.

So surrender to the reminders that take you back to reclaim what will forever belong to you—those feelings that, in their moment, were wonderful, blissful and true; all the beautiful things that you once allowed yourself to feel and do.

Go back and collect your joy, your laughter, your intimacy, your warmth, your smiles—all the special memories that made that relationship once so worthwhile—because they are yours still to keep.

And when you can reclaim how those moments made you feel in love's name, without shame or blame, without regret or remorse; perhaps even with a renewed gratitude for the love that once was—you will know that you are finally healed.

And you will know that you are ready to move on with life, beyond the pain, to live your life fully and to find true love again, because love is still the thing that makes our lives feel so alive and our dreams feel so real.

Lesson 96:
Meditation: Thanks for Forgiveness

Thank You, God, for giving me forgiveness.

Not emptiness. Not denial. Not numbness. Not bitterness. Not victimhood. Not fear. But a forgiveness that washes my heart clean and leaves it crystal clear.

And it is a gift that allows me to feel that I am real, and full, and understanding, and understood. And it propels me to move forward again as You already knew that it would.

Perfecting the Dance

And it frees me to enjoy the two greatest gifts given to me that anyone ever could—Your Love and my life.

Lesson 97:
Meditation: Prayer for a New Day

God, so often you've made a way out of no way. And I thank You for offering me the Light of this new day.

You have seen me through the good times and the bad—grew my faith, humility, love and understanding in ways I never had.

So where I might lose confidence in myself, stumbling in fear, please lift me in Your grace, Lord, to remind me that You are here.

And as I walk through this new day,
this is my humble prayer:

I know You. I love You. I need You. And I thank You for loving me and always being there.

Amen.

Dr. Nesha Jenkins-Tate

Lesson 98:
Affirmation: I am Built for Love

I've forgiven those who didn't know to love me well. And I got up even stronger every time I fell.

And my heart and my head now share a mutual trust. And I place God first because now I simply must.

On my journey, I face the bitter and I embrace the sweet. For I've learned that I can bounce back from any defeat.

And I release the past to return it to the One above. Because I know now that I was only built for Love.

NOTES

NOTES

Chapter 9

Happiness

*Don't wait to find love. Let love find you,
fully alive and actively giving
joy to a life that you already enjoy living.*

*Every awakened ear longs to hear
its highest calling.
Every human soul has others in the fold
that it must reach.
Every blessing is both a test and a testimony.
Every culture has learned some lessons
that it must teach.
And when we graciously answer our calling;
and when we teach and touch other lives;
and when we can humbly confess
the many ways we've been blessed—
all those things invariably bring us
the highest joy and happiness.*

Chapter 9
Happiness

Lesson 99: Dancing with Life as It Comes Your Way
Lesson 100: Fuel for Every Journey
Lesson 101: Taking Chances
Lesson 102: Healing a Homesick Soul
Lesson 103: I only Fear my own Despair
Lesson 104: Hope is your Light
Lesson 105: A Hunger for Love
Lesson 106: Built and Born to Thrive
Lesson 107: Old Age Loves a Sage
Lesson 108: Affirmation: I am One of God's fruits
Lesson 109: Affirmation: I am Touched
Lesson 110: Affirmation: I am Affirming Life
Lesson 111: Affirmation: I am Renewed
Lesson 112: Affirmation: I am Still
Lesson 113: Meditation: Playing your Song

Perfecting the Dance

Lesson 99:
Dancing with Life as It Comes Your Way

Let's dance through this journey across all of Life's miles—our sorrows outweighed by our laughter and smiles.

Not sleepwalkers but dancers, vibrantly alive and awake—giving away more of our love than we dare try to take.

And no matter how long in each moment we stay, let's keep dancing with Life as it comes our way.

And when we arrive at a place that is earthbound no more, let's say we left our hearts back there on the dance floor—because that's what we believed our hearts were meant for.

·•❋❋❋•·

Lesson 100:
Fuel for Every Journey

Hope was born in the moment of our conception. Across time, it fuels our will to live.

When that single sperm, among the many, races ahead of the multitude to carry forth the good news of the coming of life, it ignites a path of light in a warm and fertile space—filling that space with the hope that a new soul is coming into this place to fulfill another mission of the Creator's eternal Grace.

And when our mission is complete, which only our Creator can best assess—perhaps Hope transforms into a heavenly path to guide the Soul back home to rest.

Dr. Nesha Jenkins-Tate

So our mission, in the life for which we've been given breath, is to line this hopeful path between birth and death with stepping stones of light and love and happiness.

Lesson 101:
Taking Chances

It is
not destiny,
not doctrine,
not choice,
but Chance

that teaches us best how to rely on the divine dance between fate and faith—

perhaps even in ways that our religions never will, for a fully pre-scripted life is a life not likely fulfilled.

So remember to create enough time and space, in all of your worldly plans, to feel the spontaneous combustions of Grace, sent as miracles and gifts through Chance.

Lesson 102:
Healing a Homesick Soul

Have you ever sunk into a place of sadness so bleak that parts of your soul seemed to speak of longing to return back home to the Heavens?

Have you ever felt so low on love and so lacking in purpose that your soul longed to be joyfully nurtured by the loving unity and peace that it knew at first, before falling into the muddy dustiness of this new earth?

Well, that is what I call a "homesick soul." And when your soul feels homesick, it will start to recede—leaving you slipping into a darkness that causes your whole heart to bleed.

And while true that may be, you must never let your soul get ahead of your destiny—for now is your time to live.

So when your soul feels homesick, instead of trying to hold yourself together by holding on to the dismal feelings you also long to flee, sometimes you might need to mend your heart and cleanse your soul by setting parts of your spirit free.

It might mean crying so hard that it leaves you slimy, swollen, ugly and drained—like an infant in a fetal ball, after a near-fatal fall, where no one heard and no one came.

It might mean screaming out so loudly from your core that you awaken all the souls who love you behind Heaven's door, as they cry with you and pray that your soul will ache no more.

It might mean opening up your soul so widely that you fall to your knees as you call out to God to, just please, help you to shed all the painful tattered pieces so they can't hurt you like before.

And as you release the parts of your soul that no longer serve you well here on earth, it can feel like a new-birth. It can leave you in a lighter space to heal. It can transform you to a better place to feel all the Love that has always been all around you all the time.

So never let your soul get ahead of your destiny, for this earth now is your home. And flowers planted here by God can grow and blossom, even through concrete and stone.

For it is your divine time right now to be alive. And you are never alone.

· · ✲✵✲ · ·

Lesson 103:
I only Fear my own Despair

In all my loving reverence, it isn't God that I fear—for I know God to be my light and my love who will eternally be near. So it is myself that I fear when, in my own despair, I turn away from God's Light to explore the depths of my soul through a valley of darkness.

Yet, invariably He speaks to my heart as He covers my sight, saying: "It is time now to turn away from the shadows and turn toward the Light."

And when I am brave enough to obey, and humble enough to allow Him to re-mold me as His human clay, then I remember again in the depths of my soul that He is the Almighty-All and is

Perfecting the Dance

still in control; and that, with faith, I will be delivered eventually into a brighter day.

Lesson 104:
Hope is your Light

We can actually live without faith. But when hope dies, people die—or beautiful parts of them rot and die inside.

Hope is a thing we must nurture—for it has a life all its own. And the darkness of hopelessness will bind you and then blind you from seeing the true value of your own life. It will poison your heart until you can no longer impart any love toward others.

So I have learned that falling apart is a far better thing than sitting tightly wrapped while hopelessly withering away. And I have learned that it is okay to throw open my heart and let my whole world fall apart as long as I don't completely lose sight of all of my scattered pieces.

You see, once we are open enough to let in enough light to call upon peace, we can then see well enough again to re-assemble ourselves. We can pause in our peace and choose the parts of ourselves that we will embrace to move forward, while leaving behind those crumpled pieces that dared to crush us and push us into the brink of darkness.

Hope is our life-line to the Creator's voice and it guides us always to a braver choice.

Lesson 105:
A Hunger for Love

Sometimes, inadvertently, we starve ourselves of Love.

We starve ourselves by holding our breath as we watch and wait for that great soul-mate who will bring us the chance for true romance—that beautiful, delightful, intoxicating dance.

But love, real love, is always near. It comes through the kind eyes of strangers. It paints itself as a warm smile upon the human face. It comes through friends and family who care about our well-being. It comes in every breath that we take.

Breathing is our first form of lovemaking. God's gift of breath is our first and truest love.

So don't hold your breath, even as you wait and watch for romance. Take in every breath deeply. Release each breath with a passion for your life. Be reminded, as you breathe, that you are always loved.

When you overlook all the love that is around you and inside you, you carry a hungry, thirsty, breathless, broken soul into your relationships. And romance just doesn't stand a chance of filling all those voids.

Romance can take our breath away, but here's the thing: it assumes that we already knew how to breathe. So breathe in all the love that is offered to you in every moment. And fill up on love in all of its forms.

Perfecting the Dance

That way, you will have enough love to pour into your lover's cup. And even as the stardust settles around the romance, you won't ever forget that you have always been loved.

··❋❋❋··

Lesson 106:
Built and Born to Thrive

We are survivors—sent here to become thrivers.

Your soul survived the journey from your Heavenly Father into the groin of your earthly one. And when you grew tired of swimming around inside your father's sack, you swam toward your mother and grew beautifully intact, eventually pressing yourself gently against her back, to let her know that you were ready to go and see the light of day, strong enough by then to go outside her womb to play your new role in this new world.

So between her tears and primal screams, your mom blessed you and pushed you onward toward your dreams, through a middle-passage down a dark and narrow stream.

And your soul stayed feverishly alive—
until finally you had fully arrived.

Then your eyes embarked on a new journey to adjust to the light, to the twists and turns of life's stormy days and its steamy nights.

You even survived the climb of mountains so high that they allowed you to stand and look down into the eye of your valleys. And you gave thanks that your spirit hadn't drowned somewhere down there—even when things might have been unclear, when dreams dangled on the thread of an unanswered prayer.

But you didn't drown in the valleys because you knew not to dive. Instead, you grew the love inside yourself, keeping your dreams and your spirit alive.

And your Heavenly Father never ever left your side.
And isn't that the only way that each of us survives?
So today, let go and get still
and still let Him be your Guide.

For He's telling you to open your heart now,
and not your eyes—
so you can see all the wonderful blessings
all around you and deep inside.

Blessings too many of us just never see
because we remain simply content to be
a survivor—even as He tells us to let go
and know that He alone must be the driver,
guiding us to know the joys
of being built to be a thriver…

Yes.
You were built for your journey.

Yes.
You've been blessed since your birth.

Yes.
You were sent on this mission
to share your blessings with this earth.

So today breathe deeply
and release

and retrieve
and receive
all your blessings.

For you were born to love—and built to thrive.

Lesson 107:
Old Age Loves a Sage

Live your truth.
Enjoy your youth.
Love deeply with all your heart.
And never give-up before you start.

Explore the adventures that pour life into your dreams—for a lifetime can fly by so quickly, it seems.

And old-age loves a seasoned sage
who can bask regally at center-stage
and bring forward many delightful tales—
about lessons learned when we laughed and cried,
when we spoke a bold truth or brazenly lied,
when we finally succeeded or repeatedly tried.

And old-age seems to long to know
that we lived a life so rich and full,
that no room was left
for any regrets.

Lesson 108:
Affirmation: I am One of God's Fruits

If someone does or says things that offend us, and we shrink, sulk and simmer—recognize that we are allowing ourselves to be reduced to victims.

But never ever wallow in "victim-stew."

What is victim-stew? It's a murky place inside where we hide and simmer as we try to muster the courage to stand-up for ourselves.

And here's the thing. Even if eventually we do find the courage, because it was fed by victim-stew, it may be fueled by anger, not by love.

If it simmers long enough, anger can harden into resentment. It can flare-up into rage. It can mobilize into wrath—and wrath will attack anyone and anything that comes near its path. That's how victims find other human ingredients to toss into the stew.

So don't continually accept thoughtlessness. And don't allow yourself to become engulfed in pain. Speak to it directly. Then set it free.

Lovingly affirm who you are and how you want to be treated. Suggest a new way to interact. Then listen with your heart. If the person respects your request, move forward into change. But if the person resists, perhaps even rationalizing the old ugly behavior, you may need to create some space and distance where s/he can grow.

When you resist simmering in victim-stew, you grow big inside. You feel more in touch and more in love with the God-force

Perfecting the Dance

in you. You even may teach someone how to treat those they respect and love. And you can grow to see the other person in a more loving light.

AFFIRMATION:
Today I am reminded that I was not born to feel like a victim. I was born to feel valuable and valued. I am a precious fruit—for I am one of the powerful ways that God nourishes the world with His Love.

Lesson 109:
Affirmation: I am Touched

Do you know just how much we all need the human touch?

Touch is so important to the human experience that newborn babies who are left untouched and unheld over extended periods of time are more likely to sustain lower infancy weights and a higher mortality rate.

We literally need to be physically touched to prolong and improve our quality of life.

Touch reminds us that we are connected to something greater than our individual selves, that we are also connected to humanity, that we are part of the web of Love.

Handshakes, hugs, holding hands, some forms of dance, being groomed, being massaged, play-wrestling, cuddling, tickling, consensual sexual intimacy—these all enhance our quality of life through touch, which is our most intimate form of communication.

Dr. Nesha Jenkins-Tate

AFFIRMATION:
Today I am giving thanks for my community of intimates—family, friends, colleagues, caregivers, persons with whom I share fun and fellowship, and even pets. I am reminded that days need not go by without my being able to appropriately touch and be touched by another life. Touch is a thing that we all need so much. It reminds us that we are cherished and loved among the living.

Lesson 110:
Affirmation: I am Affirming Life

Depression, disease and despair
are no longer welcome here
for they only bring misery, pain, and strife.

So as I walk through this dark valley again,
I declare that the shadow is not my friend—
for this is my body, my temple, my Life.

And I walk toward Love. And I look toward Light.
And I press forward, intending to win this fight.
For today I am reclaiming my God-given right
to live and laugh and love again
in Peace.

Perfecting the Dance

Lesson 111:
Affirmation: I am Renewed

When there is only tranquility, God, and me
I can most clearly hear my highest destiny—
calling, soothing, and guiding me,
setting all of my worries free.

My journey moves now at a slower pace.
Love, peace and joy flow across my face.
I can feel God's presence in this space.
All my fears are leaving without a trace.
I am in the powerful presence of Grace.

So today I am reminded once again
that peace ultimately must begin
with faith…
with me…
within.

Lesson 112:
Affirmation: I am Still

Today I am making the time to be quiet and still, to feel myself honoring the gift of breath that is the greatest gift of life and the most abundant expression of love.

As I breathe slowly and deeply, I visualize floating across a vast ocean of gratitude. My many blessings over the years become crystal clear beneath a calm blue sea—and I can see all the moments in my life that have been most dear to me.

My still waters run wide and deep. And I am blessed even as I sleep, for I am still fully alive!

As I receive breath graciously, and release thanks abundantly, I am refreshed and renewed—for mine is a journey of the highest gratitude.

And on this vast ocean of joy, I feel divinely guided by God's will, and humbled by His mercies as my journey continues... still.

Lesson 113:
Meditation: Playing your Song

Get out of your house.
Get out of your head.
Re-open your heart.

You're alive!
Not dead.

And there's a dance-floor for you
in the palm of God's hand.

And they are playing your song
to remind you to dance!

NOTES

NOTES

PART THREE

Perfecting the Dance

We don't have to be perfect to be gifted.
We don't have to be perfect to be wise.
We don't have to be perfect to be of service;
to serve our purpose and see dreams materialize.
We don't have to be perfect to be loved and loving;
to forgive and be forgiven
when loving truths have been denied.

For we cannot be, nor can we see,
our own perfection.
It can only be seen in our being
through God's eyes.

Chapter 10

The Purpose inside Your Soul

*Even in those moments
when you can't believe in yourself,
believe with all your heart in your purpose.*

*When the things that you hold most dearly to be true
find a way to shine through in all that you do,
you will know that you are serving your purpose.*

The hocus-pocus is in the focus.

Chapter 10
The Purpose inside Your Soul

Lesson 114:   Wake-up Call
Lesson 115:   Listen to your Calling
Lesson 116:   Purpose, Destiny, Choice and Chance
Lesson 117:   Be the Main Character in your Story
Lesson 118:   Your Vision or your Television?
Lesson 119:   Don't Block your Blessings
Lesson 120:   Living with Balance is a Challenge
Lesson 121:   How Badly do You Want It?
Lesson 122:   Forging Signatures
Lesson 123:   Beyond Your Dreams
Lesson 124:   Affirmation: I am Humbled
Lesson 125:   Affirmation: I am Singing on Purpose

Perfecting the Dance

Lesson 114:
Wake-up Call

Your peace and fulfillment can never be grasped—
while eavesdropping on someone else's calling,
while sleep-walking down somebody else's path.

So it is time now to wake-up
and take up your mantle.

For the Universe is calling out to an authentic you
to deliver your gifts in the way that only you do.

So rise...
and shine!

······

Lesson 115:
Listen to your Calling

We each have a Calling.
And until we answer it,
our lives may feel unfulfilled.

Don't expect others to see it in you,
to reach inside and kindly pull it out of you.
And don't expect others to hear it for you.
They have their own callings to answer.

Our calling is not our platform to ask for love.
It is our opportunity and our privilege
to answer to love.

So accept that you may not always be granted
permission, promotion, praise, or pay.
And do it anyway.

And know that, in many ways, you will be granted
a sense of purpose and, on some days,
even a sense of peace.

Something in your soul is calling you.
Can you hear it?

Well, don't fear it.
Speak life into it.
Now, see it.
And do it!
Because only YOU can answer to it.

Don't be afraid to do your God-thing.
Deliver the gifts you were sent here to bring!

··❋❋❋··

Lesson 116:
Purpose, Destiny, Choice and Chance

Life, it seems, is this delicate dance—between Purpose, Destiny, Choice and Chance.

Purpose:
We come to this earth to serve some Purpose. And that purpose connects us in a very special way to others who share our time during this space of history. And once we own our purpose, it will help us to attract and gravitate toward kindred souls of a similar mission.

Our mission on earth comes of birth in two ways—by answering a higher calling, and by serving a higher purpose. In other words, we are called to do something here on earth so that, ultimately, that something might serve some valuable purpose in the lives of others.

Our "calling" calls us toward an occupation, career or avocation for which we have been naturally blessed with certain innate talents. The virtues woven in the fiber of our core make us built well to wear its robe. As a child, our calling might show-up in the games and roles we choose to play. As an adult, it might show-up in our hobbies, if not our careers. Our calling makes us feel more fully alive when we are engaged in it. Something outside of ourselves emboldens us to channel its energy.

For example, you might be blessed with natural talents that make you well-suited to write, teach, lead, sing, or act; to be an architect, an engineer, or any number of other vocational pursuits. If so, the career you passionately pursue in one of these fields is likely your calling.

Our "purpose," on the other hand, guides us toward a cause, a service, a community, a virtue, or even a situation for which we've been blessed with the unique life experiences to offer deeper insights. Our purpose makes us feel useful, and it makes our lives feel more meaningful, when we are serving it. It begs us to give greater life to something outside of ourselves.

Our purpose can guide us toward places where our calling can best be applied to touch other lives. It can shape the unique way in which we give ourselves to our calling.

For example, two people might be drawn toward serving the same purpose—peace-making. Yet each might be *called* to serve that purpose in a different way. One might have an innate talent for writing and might choose to become a writer, finding fulfillment by reporting on peace-keeping missions or by writing books and articles that help others to find inner-peace. The other might feel *called* to become a lawyer, finding his or her greatest fulfillment serving as an arbitrator or mediator. Different callings answered; same higher purpose served.

Here's another example involving three people. Person-A and Person-B might be drawn toward serving the same purpose—bringing greater joy and happiness into the world. Yet, each might bring forth that joy through different callings. Person-A might feel *called* to become a teacher, known for having a classroom environment of happy learners. Person-B might feel *called* to become an entertainer who makes audiences laugh through comedy. Different callings answered; same higher purpose served.

The third person in this scenario, Person-C, might share Person-A's calling to be a teacher. Yet Person-C might yearn to serve the purpose of offering more nurturing and parenting to the world—doing so then by being a teacher, especially loved for his or her nurturing presence in the classroom. Different higher purpose served; same calling answered.

Our calling is a means; our purpose is a desired end. Our calling is the vehicle; our purpose is the driver. While our calling may be our *avocation*, our purpose is our *advocation*.

And contrary to popular thinking, our higher purpose in life is never simply to make more money to grow rich. The accrual of personal wealth may be one's dream, but it is likely neither one's highest calling nor one's highest purpose. Our purpose is always bigger than merely ourselves alone. So if you've been blessed with the natural talent for attracting wealth, that talent

Perfecting the Dance

can be channeled into a calling that also serves some higher purpose.

For example, one person with the talent to attract wealth might feel called vocationally to serve as a financial advisor or a financial planner, moved by the higher purpose of helping others to grow their wealth or create long-term financial stability. Another person, with that same talent for attracting wealth, might feel called to become a fundraiser, moved by the higher purpose of helping charities so that they can expand their capacity and sustainability.

Our souls long for an alignment between calling and purpose.

Serving our calling without the sense that we are also serving our purpose can feel like an enjoyable enough personal outlet—but it also can leave us feeling incomplete, as though there is some lack of direction in our lives.

Similarly, serving our purpose without integrating that into serving our calling can allow us to feel useful—but it also can be unfulfilling, as though we recognize that we have inside us the capacity to give ourselves in a different, better or bigger way to the particular service, virtue or situation.

At various points in our lives, we may feel called to choose new ways that we can serve our higher purpose. We might feel called to different vocations or to higher progressions of the same career as we gain new life experiences and new insights.

Therefore, it is important to stay open to change. Listen to your intuition. Learn well the lessons of your past. Expand your outlook by growing the network of your community. Observe the seemingly random events that occur by chance. Make time for quiet moments when you can communicate with your

Maker. All these can serve as magnets for a compass pointing you always toward the best next direction.

Purpose also has a situational component.

There is not only a purpose for each life, but also a purpose for each day, and indeed each moment and each situation.

And have you ever noticed that when unpleasant or unplanned situations happen to us, sometimes we can only accept them if we believe that they have happened for our purpose? Immediately we try to translate the purpose of the situation into something intended to be useful to our own lives—placing ourselves at the center of the Universe around which these things presumably revolve, giving us perhaps some sense of benefit and control.

But while situational things may happen for some purpose, the truth is, it's not always for our purpose. Sometimes we are merely there to serve the purpose; the situational purpose is not there to serve us.

Sometimes things happen for the good of someone else and the Creator places us there merely as characters in a story that serves another life, perhaps a life being shown a better way to make choices.

That is why even the biggest thinkers need to be also grounded in the present moment. That is why we mustn't totally exclusively focus on the grand scheme of our life's purpose; on the career or calling for which we are being financially compensated; or on the big things we are working toward that will unfold in the future.

Perfecting the Dance

Instead, we also must be present in the moment to recognize the everyday situations when we can make a difference by spontaneously serving some positive purpose we are being called toward in the present moment, in a perhaps unexpected situation.

Our calling and our purpose must be lived in the present moment and not just nurtured, stored and planned for some future grand reveal. Otherwise, we may miss some growth and sharing opportunities along the way.

We each are here to serve some higher purpose or purposes, and how that plays out moment by moment on a daily basis, in various situations, also is heavily influenced by three other aspects—by destiny, by our choices, and by chance.

Destiny:
Destiny is that divine plan that influences the course of our lives. It is fate.

For example, there may be people we feel destined to have met, drawn into each other's space as if by the magnetic influence of fate. And when that happens in matters of the heart, sometimes we assume that the person was brought into our lives as a soul-mate. Maybe so. But even if so, sometimes soul-mates stay and sometimes they move away—even as we still can choose to keep them in our hearts forever.

When destiny brings people together, not always as lovers but even sometimes as friends, each person still gets to choose whether and how s/he wants to stay in the other person's life. Destiny will not negate the free-will we have to choose who we keep close.

Perhaps destiny even has its own way of adapting to the range of choices we might make. Think of it as a kind of big "nested-if" phenomenon. If we choose this way or that way, or if we choose not to choose at all, then destiny has already predetermined a course of response. Perhaps, it can adjust any course while holding the destination constant to accommodate any possible human choice or chosen path.

And perhaps Karma is that part of destiny that we co-create; a way of invoking lessons aligned with higher laws that respond to our choices, a way of keeping the greater balance from being disrupted when we don't choose wisely or lovingly.

Choice:
We are not pre-programmed robots. We are not solely instinctive creatures. We are volitional beings. We've been granted the power of choice, the gift of free-will.

That means that we can choose; we can observe and analyze our own choices; and we can even change our minds and choose differently at any point in time. We are free to make choices about our lives every moment of everyday.

So even while we are called here to serve some purpose on earth, ultimately we still have a choice about how we give ourselves in service to that purpose.

Natural talents and the things about which we feel passionately may give us some indication of how to best serve our calling. But whether we choose to act upon our calling in a positive way, a negative way, or not at all—by the divine design of destiny, that purpose shall be served.

So we can choose to serve either as a source of inspiration or as an example of poor choices; as a main character, or in a supporting role. But life goes on and there will be other vessels who can be called to meet the needs of the moment for the greater good. Perhaps they can't do it in the same special way that we could, but if the greater need is crucial, the need will be met by another vessel.

Our choices may be evident in the physical realm. But they also may be invisible—on an energy level that is fueled by our intentions, our beliefs, our expectations and our sense of self. All these influence the energy we attract and call forth in others and the situations that manifest themselves repeatedly in our lives. Our choices create our patterns.

And while the Creator has given us the gift of free will, He also is ever present in our lives to lend guidance—through our intuition, our conscience, our calling, our relationships, and through every circumstance—and all of these blessings can help to inform our decisions in life, as we dance.

And as long as human beings are free to make choices, some of our choices will randomly collide with the choices of others. Sometimes that will lead to conflicts and chaos—but sometimes it also will create a space for chance.

Chance:
Chance is that fertile field of random events that is not restricted by anyone's plans—not time's nor The Divine's; and not yours nor mine. Chance is a space for spontaneous choices. It combines all the elements of the moment and rattles them like dice to reveal a unique chemistry.

But most importantly, that space that we call "chance" is a place where God often reminds us that He is not confined by even His own divine plans. It is a place where He reminds us that, as a living God, He has the ultimate free-will and the upper-hand.

God isn't dead and He isn't in hiding. He didn't stop talking, listening, seeing and guiding when the scribes put down their sacred pens some thousands of years ago. He remains eternally alive and is actively in the flow.

So as the choreographer of seven billion dancers, He can elevate or override any purpose, any choice, any chance-encounter, or natural law. He can swirl things around until lost souls are found; until mere human beings are enlightened and heightened by His awe.

He can introduce something so utterly devastating that it humbles us and compels us to huddle together as human-family and be still. Or, He can intervene with something timed so perfectly that we have no choice but to see it as a *miracle* of God's own will.

And chance loves to dance in the garment of miracles.

As human beings, often we prefer to disregard the possibilities of chance because chance makes us feel out of control. We no longer can rely on the known laws of cause and effect. And it can displace us from that selfish little place where each of us tends to feel that we belong—at the center of the Universe around which all other things revolve.

Yet, chance is perhaps that most fertile place—where lives are spared by the intervention of Grace; where prayers find their answers in a sacred space; and where God still reminds us He's in charge of this place.

Meaning:
So Life, it seems, is this beautiful dance between Purpose, Destiny, Choice and Chance. And the real beauty and the duty of that cosmic romance is to remind us that whether things happen on purpose; by the pull of destiny; by our own choices; or

Perfecting the Dance

by the whimsy of chance—we still can choose to glean our own meaning from what we feel inside each moment, as we dance.

And *meaning* is the music that can uplift every Soul and inspire, taking each journey a lot further, and just a little bit higher.

Lesson 117:
Be the Main Character in your Story

You've got a story.
I've got a story.
Everybody's got a story.

Yet it's not the story,
but the "character"
that has evolved out of the story,
that makes our story so worth sharing.

Character.

It is the thicker spine that you grew.
It is the bigger person that you grew into.
It is the self that propels you to follow-through.
It is the soulful one who knows exactly what to do
to console the fearful one who, even today,
still comes to visit you.

Your character is your core.
And who can dare ask you for more?

Lesson 118:
Your Vision or your Television?

A vision without a plan is like a television. You can sit on your sofa, imagine how things are staged, tell others all about it, and feel totally engaged—with no evidence whatsoever of its reality in your life.

So yes, have a vision. And yes, keep on dreaming. But shepherd them by binding them to a higher purpose with a deeper meaning.

Seek guidance and wisdom from others, foremost and frequently from God. And don't run away when all the little things seem to get just a little too hard. Give yourself permission to fail, to fumble, to fall. But take a stand by having a plan to keep guiding you purposely toward your highest call.

Surely, there will be twists, turns, detours and lessons along the way. And you may even have to serve sometimes without gratitude or pay. But if you are moving your feet, and not just daydreaming in your seat, you are bound to make some great things happen.

Because here's the deal: Our dreams and visions long for us to get up and make them real.

Lesson 119:
Don't Block your Blessings

Procrastination, doubt and pessimism can seem like the shield to protect your heart from the pain it might feel if you were disappointed by dreams that failed to become real.

But there is no reason to enter a new season with the spirit of doubt in your eyes—when you and God can handle any disappointments, should they ever arise—as you are learning about discerning your blessings, even the ones that might wear a disguise.

Always offer to each new thing your best. And of all things, expect nothing less. For you deserve to serve your highest purpose and to also know that you are blessed.

So trust what you feel
and put down your shield
and open that door that can finally reveal
a path toward your many blessings.

Lesson 120:
Living with Balance is a Challenge

Dizzily I dance between deprivation and gluttony, painfully struck by the same old epiphany—that living a life of balance is still my biggest challenge.

The Soul aspires toward ascension. And sometimes that tug, that calling toward a dream, can become discomforting, for so often it may seem that it constantly compels us to do something bigger.

So perhaps the little dance we do between low and high extremes gives us that chance to feel a false sense of transformation—where living a life of balance may not.

What happens to that dream when it is deferred? Some believe that it will implode. But sometimes I wonder what happens to dreams actualized? Do they then actually explode?

And is our fear of that dream-explosion, on a scale perhaps of greatness, the thing that keeps us zig-zagging between extremes?

Can't stop because we fear failure. Can't start because we fear success. Or so, sometimes, it seems.

And if we believe that "the good die young" and we aspire to live long, do we then become fearful of doing good?

…Yet, maybe the good only die young metaphorically, unafraid to repeatedly die and re-birth themselves toward a greater good.

And perhaps it really doesn't matter whether we arrive at a place of balance in our lives, but merely that we arrive at a place of courage—where there may not be a total absence of fear but there is a firm will to persevere through it.

Courage.

It can make us so unafraid of failure, so unimpressed by success, that we humbly serve our highest purpose, and boldly reveal our true greatness. And perhaps then we can clearly see a wonderful new epiphany:

Perfecting the Dance

That the place of balance we are seeking is actually *joy* and joy comes when we feel purposeful, meaningful, centered and whole—not necessarily in our lives but verily in our souls.

For only from there can this truth-guiding question periodically unfold: *Do these things sit well within my soul?*

··❊❋❊··

Lesson 121:
How Badly do You Want It?

Sometimes we need a good sobering "aha" moment to recognize when we've had one too many "ha-ha" moments that might be leading us down the path of a major "uh-uh" moment.

So yes, we should keep our eyes on the prize but we must never be so enamored with the promise and the purpose that we disregard the process that might be required to fulfill them.

A process is a special kind of journey. It will challenge you and stretch you repeatedly, all the while asking: "How badly really do you want this?" And if repeatedly you can answer with conviction: "I want this badly, still"—then it will drive you to keep on pushing and following through with clear focus and sheer will.

A process requires that we not only *go* through it, but ultimately that we also *grow* through it—for it is the growing that makes us fit, even in our own eyes, for the prize.

Consciously exercising the body is a great way to strengthen one's will and spiritual fitness. Physical movement can be a metaphor that gives us a sense of facing life's challenges, pressing forward, and progressing through them. It can give us a sense of accomplishment.

It moves energy around inside the body and releases energy that no longer serves us well. It plants us firmly in the present moment and builds gratitude for the gift of life. It teaches us the importance of proper breathing, especially in the face of adversity. It teaches us the power of commitment.

You see, commitment is not about convenience. Commitment is about courage—the courage to recognize that which is inside you. It keeps you pushing through your potential to reach your promise, toward effectively serving your purpose. Courage is a thing we can carry deeply inside; but only when it shows up in our lives and in the lives of others, can we recognize courage as bravery. And your will is the spine that supports your courage.

So move through life from the center of your soul. Own your energy. Own your peace. Own your physical presence. Own your power.

Being peaceful does not mean being passive and inconclusive. Being powerful does not mean being aggressive and abusive. You are here to be purposeful. And being on purpose means being at peace with using your power to propel the dream into positive action.

Indeed, sometimes we may have to learn how to dance with webbed feet before we can grow the wings we'll need for flying. But the key always is to keep on trying.

And the hocus-pocus is in the focus that we bring toward serving our purpose.

Perfecting the Dance

Lesson 122:
Forging Signatures

Everybody who has your same name will not have your same signature. When they sign the name you share, it won't look the same as when you sign it.

That's because your signature is a unique song from your soul. It is a tribute to the character you allow the Soul to bear while it is here on earth.

Your written signature; your fingerprints; your style; the melody in your laughter; the special way that you breathe life into your talents to make them gifts... All of these are unique expressions of your soul—your soul's signature.

They remind you that, while you are one with the multitude, it is important to realize that you remain very special in the Creator's eyes.

So never envy or imitate what is special in someone else—because that is the same as forging someone's signature.

And never deny what is special in you—because that is the same as refusing to sign on the bottom-line of an edict giving you permission to live your life.

When you embrace your own soul's signature, you can forge ahead with leaving your unique mark on the world.

And your signature makes it plainly clear that you recognize exactly why you are here.

· • ❋ ❋ ❋ • ·

Lesson 123:
Beyond Your Dreams

Believing in your dreams is important. It helps you to focus your energies on achieving a personal goal.

But if you aren't careful, your dreams and goals can become self-absorbing and your ego might even incline you toward seeking wealth or fame merely for the sake of same.

Maybe we were sent here to deliver more to life than just our vanity and to make more of life than just our money.

And if that is so, then believing in one's "purpose" is perhaps even more powerful than believing in one's "dreams."

Knowing that you have a purpose can propel you to look beyond yourself to identify where and how your gifts and talents can best serve others. It's okay to profit from serving our purpose but the profit should not be the driver so much as the need to share the gifts we were given to share.

When we leave this earth, we can't take any of our profits with us, but we can take all the gifts we brought that remained unused because we simply refused to share them.

And while our dreams can sometimes leave us stuck in a dreamland, our purpose almost always propels us to take action. Knowing that we have a purpose for being alive, at this

Perfecting the Dance

appointed time, in this body, can fuel us with hope because it gives our lives meaning.

Believing in your dreams requires that you believe in yourself. Not bad sometimes, but not always enough.

Believing in your purpose, on the other hand, requires that you believe in something bigger than yourself. And that can take an incredible weight off your shoulder because you know then that there is Someone greater to whom you can turn for guidance because that Someone greater believed in you and entrusted you to share your gifts.

Knowing that awesome truth, we can just keep on striving to live our lives on purpose—beyond even our wildest dreams!

Lesson 124:
Affirmation: I am Humbled

If God made everything, from beyond the sky to beneath the bottom of the sea—just who on earth am "I" to dare question what God can make of "me?"

AFFIRMATION:
Today I will move out of my own way and allow my Creator to hold me, mold me and unfold me—for I am a living testimony of His Grace.

Dr. Nesha Jenkins-Tate

Lesson 125:
Affirmation: I am Singing on Purpose

If humanity is God's choir, what is your song?

What are the gifts that you were sent here to share with others? Metaphorically speaking, what are the songs that you can sing into the world to help you to feel most purposeful and peaceful?

In the Creator's mass choir, there are billions of singers and many songs to be sung. What is the song you are being asked to sing? Perhaps you carry a song that supports virtues and values in one of the following keys of life—toward offering the world more:

Artistry, Beauty, Clarity, Community, Courage, Creativity, Discovery, Empowerment, Faith, Freedom, Gracefulness, Guidance, Harmony, Healing, Hope, Hospitality, Humor, Inspiration, Intervention, Inventiveness, Joy, Justice, Knowledge, Leadership, Love, Nourishment, Nurturing, Order, Parenting, Peace, Perseverance, Resilience, Restoration, Transformation, Truth, Unity, Vision, Wealth, Wisdom…

So listen to your heart and hear *your* song. Then sing it by finding ways that you can translate your song into actions that mobilize your purpose toward having a positive impact on the world.

To illustrate: Suppose that your song (your life's purpose) is to bring the world greater Harmony. You might, then, choose or feel called to translate that song into actions that touch other people's lives through any of several ways that are compatible with your natural talents—as a musician; a composer; a poet; a designer; a stylist; or even a diplomat who brings harmony between opposing factions.

Perfecting the Dance

Your natural talents and your life experiences will help in guiding your choices.

But as you sing on purpose, be particularly attuned to the lessons to be gained from high-titles, fortune and fame—for they can become distractions if you don't incorporate them into serving your mission.

If you are granted *high-titles* in the process, consider that perhaps you are simply being called to a place of greater influence where you can open doors more widely to help others walk through them. Perhaps you are being granted a platform from which you can uplift others who might be more inclined then to listen.

If you are granted *fortune* in the process, consider that perhaps you are simply being called to a place of greater benevolence where you can create more hope for others and more opportunities for others to recognize and share their gifts, too.

If you are granted *fame* in the process, consider that perhaps you are simply being called to a place of greater responsibility where you can serve as an example, touching lives and uplifting hearts among a mass of people with your insights and gifts.

So as you answer your calling and deliver your gifts, recognize these cosmic shifts for what they might be. Avoid the distractions of the ego that can cause you to start humming along because you've forgotten the importance of the words of your song; or that can cause you to start singing loudly off-key because you've started to believe that only you have the right to carry that tune.

AFFIRMATION:
Today I can hear so clearly the song the Creator placed in my heart and I am singing my song to the world. I don't need to

audition. I don't need to compete. I don't need to compare. I just need to be the gifted soul entrusted with this song, making the world a little better because I am delivering my gifts.

So today I am gladly singing that glorious song that I've been humming in my soul for far too long.

And each time that I set my song free, I can feel the God of Peace here with me... smiling.

NOTES

NOTES

Chapter 11

The Language of New Leaders

*Convey a vision so compellingly large and clear—
that even when you cannot be there,
the movement toward the vision continues.*

*Beauty opens eyes. Brilliance opens minds.
Personality opens hearts. Character opens doors.
But Faith can move mountains.*

*We are well-built to bear our burdens
and we are well-blessed to bear our gifts.
So we need not waver, for God grants us no favor
that He hasn't built us to handle,
with one hand planted in His.*

Chapter 11
The Language of New Leaders

Lesson 126:   A Greater Good
Lesson 127:   Leaders Follow Leaders
Lesson 128:   Standing Center Stage
Lesson 129:   Optimist, Pessimist, Realist, Catalyst
Lesson 130:   Who do You Think You are?
Lesson 131:   You are a Promise
Lesson 132:   What Works at Work won't Work Here
Lesson 133:   Take the High Road
Lesson 134:   12 Lessons Great Leaders Learn
Lesson 135:   Affirmation: I am Greatness

Perfecting the Dance

Lesson 126:
A Greater Good

There are few things more selfish or even sadder
than wanting to climb that aspirational ladder
without also wanting to learn how to lead.

Because when we know how to competitively climb,
but we don't know how to courageously lead,
it calls into question whether our goal is
the greater good—
or just an insatiable personal greed.

So as we climb,
let's make the time
to uplift others.

And even if you struggle with
believing in God,
believe in Good
and you will ignite His presence.

··✺✸✺··

Lesson 127
Leaders Follow Leaders

Everybody is a leader—
once we recognize and commit our lives
to serving our highest purpose.

And those who you think are merely your followers?
Just know that they also

were born to be leaders
on a path that is their own calling.

You see…
On some things, we lead.
On some things, we follow.
It is a dance that lends nobility,
humility, and character to power.

Lesson 128:
Standing Center Stage

Sometimes the best way to prepare yourself for a big moment that places you at center-stage is simply to stage yourself by getting centered in your soul.

Then it is no longer about you, your fears, your dreams, your face—as you ask God to infuse you and to use you as a clear channel for His Grace.

For once we are able to *remove* ourselves, we no longer feel compelled to *prove* ourselves to anyone but the Creator, the One who can guide us from above.

And creatively, we are then freed to touch other lives and plant bountiful seeds—for as we learn to concede to God's needs, we become a manifestation of His Love.

Lesson 129:
Optimist, Pessimist, Realist, Catalyst

Some of us are Optimists:
We can see the positive side of anything. Our biggest weakness, though, is that we can sometimes be gullible, naïve, opportunistic and unprepared. Yet, Optimists are the masters of gratitude, brilliance and resilience. And when moved to serve a greater cause, Optimists are natural Nurturers.

Some of us are Pessimists:
We can see the negative side of anything. Our biggest fear is disappointment, so sometimes we can be so cautious and cynical that we miss out on amazing opportunities. Yet, Pessimists are the masters of planning, preparation and mitigation. And when moved to serve a greater cause, Pessimists are naturals at Diagnosis.

Some of us are Realists:
We can see whatever currently resides inside the heart of anything, even as the thing changes. Our biggest fear is fraud and deception, so we may sometimes lack imagination and we might even lack faith, as faith requires an appetite for trusting in things unseen. Yet Realists are the masters of clarity and discernment. And when moved to serve a greater cause, Realists are natural Healers.

Some of us are Catalysts:
We can see through anything to see the potential in its soul. Then we seek to ignite a fire to help the thing to rise higher. Our biggest weakness, though, is intruding on other people's lives, violating their right to choose the level of self at which they want to live. Yet Catalysts are the masters of deep insight and inspiration. They understand the intimacy and agency between

cause and effect. And when moved to serve a higher cause, Catalysts are natural Transformers.

So, whose outlook is best—the Optimist, the Pessimist, the Realist, or the Catalyst?

Perhaps none are better and all are needed.

The world needs people who feel joyful and exalted, especially when they can do well while helping others to feel and do well. The world needs people who are passionate about troubleshooting to help us uncover what is ailing our souls or standing between us and excellence.

The world needs people who enjoy being of service toward helping us to fix the things that are causing us to not do well and to heal the things that are causing us to not feel well. And certainly, the world needs people who themselves feel elated when they can help us to see beyond our past and current circumstances so that we can chase and embrace greater possibilities.

So the key perhaps is to know your own tendency and to try to operate from its highest frequency. Equally important is the need to welcome and maintain, in your circle of intimates, others who see things differently and who know that you are open to them offering you an alternate and perhaps balanced view.

And in my own catalytic eyes, I imagine the real lesson lies in one's ability to recognize the pitfalls you can stumble into when you rely solely on the way things are viewed in your soul as they flow through you.

Perfecting the Dance

We each need each other—in order to see how we can best be ourselves.

Lesson 130:

Who do You Think You are?

Sometimes the direction in which you are called will rub against the grain. Yet you were built to leap across the adversity and the pain; to rise above desolate dusty paths; to smell the coming of rain.

For when we are obedient to the direction in which Grace is calling, we need not fear falling.

And the question is not:
How fast can you go how far?

The question is but:
Who exactly do you think you are?

And the answer is this:
You are a child of God, and God has raised the bar.

So keep on dancing with Grace—
even as the wind hits your face.
And remember that it is absolutely no mistake
that you have been called now to dare to take
those powerful leaps
of faith.

Lesson 131:
You are a Promise

Greatness doesn't always have to roar.
Sometimes it's silent. Sometimes it whispers.
But always it is channeling love
toward serving its highest purpose.

Greatness doesn't always look brave.
Sometimes it might even look nervous.
But always it is pressing forward, daring
to be of greater service.

Greatness doesn't always stand in the spotlight.
Sometimes it kneels alone in the darkness.
But always it is shining its inner-light
toward revealing a brighter promise.

When we serve our purpose, we fulfill our promise—which is to walk the highest path we possibly can toward our greatness.

Lesson 132:
What Works at Work won't Work Here

Sometimes the roles we play so well in our vocational lives carry over unfavorably in our personal relationships. The personality traits that have paved the way for us to be leaders in our profession often are the ones that create the biggest roadblocks in our personal relationships.

Indeed, our loved ones require us to acknowledge them as fallible equals who have an unconditional place in our hearts. Our colleagues at work do not. Thus, characteristics that make us great leaders in the workplace often are not characteristics that necessarily endear us to our intimates.

To illustrate, let's look at some of the salient traits across professions and how those same habits and traits can get in the way of intimacy if we are not careful and mindful about carrying them over inappropriately.

Accountants: They often keep count of things, strive to keep books balanced, and focus on the bottom-line. However, that can promote a tit-for-tat kind of thinking that, when carried over into intimate relationships, can block the natural flow of gratitude and giving.

Athletes: They often thrive in a competitive environment and tend to have a youthfulness that fuels their greatness and popularity as players of the game. However, that competitive spirit and playful mindset, when applied to personal relationships, can sometimes show up as a lack of focus and commitment that doesn't serve well toward sustaining a long-term committed relationship.

Entertainers and Performers: They may thrive on the energy exchanged with an audience while they are on stage. However, that need to be the center of attention and to draw on the energy of others can be taxing to intimates off-stage on a routine daily basis. They may need the collective energy of a group to feed their spirits and may be challenged with feeling joyful when trying to draw on the energy of a single person or a small group of intimates.

Lawyers: They inspect evidence, try to minimize liability, and strive to win arguments. However, that scrutiny, that aim for competitive one-upmanship, and the desire to match wits to win fights can undermine a long-term relationship that requires mutual understanding, compromise and vulnerability to promote intimacy.

Clergy: They may speak to their followers from a podium or a pulpit. They are authoritative vessels who bring forth the holy lessons and messages of their faith. But a habit of speaking to other human beings from that stance can promote a holier-than-thou presence that does not translate well in private settings between equal adults. Others may feel reluctant to embark on the level of sharing needed to promote friendship and intimacy with them. And conversely, they may feel reluctant to do deep level sharing with others, fearful that they will be judged especially critically.

Teachers: They evaluate whether answers are right or wrong, whether students have learned their lessons well and where others stand on some evaluative scale. But that habit of lecturing and comparing, then rating and ranking others against some acceptable standard might feel demanding or condescending in personal matters. It might encourage competition, as loved ones vie to gain favor or escape judgment. It might also make it difficult to admit when they themselves are wrong in personal matters, because being wrong equates to having failed some evaluative test.

Trouble-shooters and Problem-solvers: They may pride themselves on being useful by identifying defects and fixing them. But then, as human beings, we are prone to being the embodiment of many quirks and "defects." So that habit of critically pointing out things perceived as broken and then trying to fix them, when carried over into personal matters, might be distancing and love-diminishing in intimate relationships.

Visual Artists: They may look for beauty and try to bring forth evidence of it by capturing it in some physical manifestation.

Perfecting the Dance

But that tendency to focus on the physical manifestation of beauty, which in itself is subjective, can cause them to objectify other human beings, placing an unusually high importance on physical appearances. Thus, they may operate at a shallow level in relationships, neglecting sometimes to notice characteristics that speak more deeply and sustainably of inner-beauty.

Of course these are all caricatures—exaggerated portraits of some of the characteristics of each of these professions. And certainly this sampling falls short of the many vocations and their roles and responsibilities across the gamut. However, they are merely offered to suggest a way to think about this matter to determine whether there is some truthfulness to this perspective that can be useful to your life.

So try making a list of the top three to five characteristics that make you great at your line of work; and then consider whether and how those same characteristics show up in your intimate relationships; and consider also whether that is working well for you and for other parties involved.

The point here is simply this: we must be mindful of imposing the habits that work so well at work onto our personal relationships.

How we show-up professionally and how we show-up personally in our relationships is a matter of mindfulness about what parts of us are most appropriately needed in each setting, in order to sustain and grow the healthiest relationships.

Below are ten (10) guideposts that can help us to remain mindful as we make shifts over the course of the day across our many roles:

1. Maintain a sense of humor. Take your roles and responsibilities seriously but not yourself.

2. Own your energy: be aware of your impact and influence on other people who are in your company.

3. Be willing to listen and learn from anyone.

4. Be sensitive to the needs of the present moment.

5. Treat your home as a sacred space for family and friends. When you must work at home, establish boundaries that don't bleed heavily into your private life.

6. Forgive yourself and everyone for everything. At home and at work, don't carry clutter in your heart. Clutter chokes creativity, productivity and intimacy.

7. Know that your soul is greater than your role. What you do is never totally who you are. Not in any setting. And this is equally true of others, too.

8. Make time for down-time. Play-time reminds you of who you are authentically in your soul. Try to allow the beauty of that authenticity to show-up across your roles. Then, perhaps the shift from a role in the workplace to your role in a private space won't feel so radical.

9. Have faith in something bigger than yourself. It will remind you that you are never alone; that you are loved and supported by the Universe; and that you don't sit at the center of it all.

10. Then finally, make and keep commitments. It is not only important to serve your purpose and your profession; it is also important to serve the people you love most.

Lesson 133:
Take the High Road

When meanness poses as manliness,
when mean-girls posture as women,
a leader pauses in peace
and extends a mirror to offer a glance
so that others might see themselves
and choose to elevate their own dance
into movement that speaks of their grace.

But as a leader decides to rise and shine
above the ugliness and the noise
of the naysayers,

s/he can hear so clearly the voice of the Divine,
guiding the course and the courage
of each way-seer.

And s/he can waltz favorably
through the fire with no fear—
through even the darkest hours where
lesser souls would crawl or stumble.

And s/he can wear a calm face
centered in a strong faith
that the high road
keeps its leaders
divinely guided and humble.

Lesson 134:
12 Lessons Great Leaders Learn

1. **Carry the dignity of the role you serve.**

Expect the best from others, yet allow people to look up to you if they need to. Sometimes that can help them to find their own strengths; sometimes it will remind you that you need to find yours again. But never look down upon or talk down toward any human being. Your situational role may be superior—but you are not.

2. **Let people know they matter.**

Remember that the people are as important as the vision and their lives are as important as the group's mission. Let people know that you care about them as human beings, and not just as through-puts who produce outputs, and they will be inspired to elevate their performance to meet the needs of the team.

3. **Inclusiveness builds and bonds a team.**

Good leaders bring people together to take them further and higher. Truth, transparency, diversity, and authenticity are attributes they admire because their teams are built on a foundation of trust across diverse talents and perspectives.

4. **See the light in the souls of others.**

Encourage others to shine their light to support the team. People want to feel essential and valuable to the mission. Allow them the leeway to bring themselves authentically to the tasks at hand. People want to feel that they are also serving their life's purpose. A good leader recognizes that and helps others realize their highest potential while helping the team to achieve its goals. Good leaders groom more good leaders.

5. Run from nothing; march toward something.

A leader focuses the team on the places they're trying to go to instead of dwelling on the places they're trying to leave. Otherwise, that old place and those old ways will simply follow the team. A leader outlines a plan that can serve as a bridge between old and new worlds.

6. Even when you cannot conquer fear, you can still master courage.

The most important characteristic of a good leader is courage. Not fearlessness, but courage—a willingness, even in the face of fear and uncertainty, to push through and guide the team forward. It means being willing to recognize and address ugliness in spirit and character while reminding people of their capacity for goodness and greatness. It also means protecting your team's spirit and your own spirit from the damage of exposure to persistently negative forces.

7. Convey a vision that is compellingly large and clear.

If your vision is compellingly large and clear, then even when you cannot be there, your team will keep on moving forward toward the goal. Allow team members to see themselves as a part of that future-state, clear that they will not be deemed obsolete by the new vision, and they will bring the best parts of themselves to the journey, knowing that they, too, will realize some of their own dreams.

8. Respect and value human dignity.

There is dignity in every role on the team, no matter where it might fall on the organizational chart. Let people know that they are needed and valued. And if there is no dignity in a role, then it is time to get rid of that role and allow the people serving those roles to do bigger things of greater value to the mission.

9. **Listen. Listen. Listen.**

Recognize that there are many voices who can help to inform the choices you ultimately will be required to make as a leader. Listening—to your God, your gut, the insights of your team, the lessons learned by peers and predecessors—each will give you a window into many perspectives who share and care about your mission. The lone-voice leader who feels compelled to impose silence as a badge of allegiance is committing a passive act of violence against the human spirit. S/He is also undermining the success of the mission.

10. **Foster an environment of respect.**

Respect should flow up and down and across the ranks and rungs of your organization. Social-climbers and organizational-climbers, who kiss-up as they spit-down and kick-across, are the leadership role-models of a dysfunctional past.

Encourage your team members to sit down and talk with each other respectfully when they need to work through differences, to learn to listen to each other with a focus on what's best for the shared mission. Discourage back-biting, in-fighting and escalations that are merely negative acts of one-upmanship that undermine trust and group cohesiveness.

Fear endears no one. But transparency, respect and love will inspire people to work together, reaching beyond and above, to advance a shared mission.

Perfecting the Dance

11. **Own the power of your influence.**

Encourage and empower people during their works-in-progress but thank and praise them only once the work actually has been done.

Encourage work-in-progress: "I understand you're doing a great job supporting the team with ABC. Please continue to keep up the good work!" Then give praise and personal thanks more publicly once the work actually has been completed: "Thank you for doing a great job supporting the team with ABC. Because of your efforts, we now can do XYZ."

If you thank individuals for every little contribution made each step of the way before they fulfill their share of obligations and responsibilities to the team, people sometimes will start to behave as though they are doing you a personal favor. Your role as leader might then be diminished to the role of a beggar gaining favors; or their ongoing performance can become tied to getting that periodic "fix" of praise from you.

Hold people accountable for contributing their results to the team. Create an environment where people feel comfortable sharing the truth about what is reasonably feasible. Seek periodic updates to assess whether the team is still moving toward the mission and to let them know that you're still interested and committed. Encourage and affirm teamwork. Empower and support your team in removing roadblocks. And reward them appropriately once they deliver.

12. **Lead where you feel called.**

It's going to be difficult to convince anyone to follow you down a new path or to move in the direction of a new goal about which you show no conviction. So try to lead in a space where you truly believe in the mission. Convey personal interest and passion around the team's mission and a genuine caring for the people who are on your team and it will spread across the team like wildfire. That is how leaders transform cultures.

Lesson 135:
Affirmation: I am Greatness

To be loved long after we are gone for having given our best to the things we loved most, while touching the lives of others.

That is greatness.

Our love is the only part of us that can last forever. And through it, we have the capacity for immortality, for defying death, for transcending time and space– by earning ourselves a sacred place in the heart of Love's eternal flame, a place that can remember to keep alive the sweetest embers of our name... a place where Love and Life are One, and both become the same.

AFFIRMATION:
Today I will do a bigger thing better because I am walking a path toward my greatness.

NOTES

NOTES

Chapter 12

The Soul of a Woman

*Even if you choose not to give your life
to a partner; even if you choose not to allow
your body to give birth—
you still can choose to give life to others
by offering them a sense of hope and
and a sense of self-worth...*

*When you have known women
who were grown women,
who strived to make God-guided decisions,
you can clearly recognize
when what stands before your eyes
is merely a girl still trying to find her own way.*

Chapter 12
The Soul of a Woman

Lesson 136:   Glorious is your Testimony
Lesson 137:   Know your Worth
Lesson 138:   Guardian of God's Fruits
Lesson 139:   Maternal Love is Eternal Love
Lesson 140:   A Peace of Her Soul
Lesson 141:   May You Dance, Dr. Maya
Lesson 142:   V Stands for Woman
Lesson 143:   Little Ms. BaddAzz
Lesson 144:   Meditation: Ain't too Proud to Pray
Lesson 145:   Affirmation: I am a Soldier

Perfecting the Dance

Lesson 136:
Glorious is your Testimony

Your strands of gray are your autumn glory:
it's the crown you've earned for your life-story.

Your wrinkles are the roadmap you have kept—
of places where you smiled, laughed,
worried and wept.

And your poise, your wisdom,
your beauty, your laughter?

All are coins in the pot of gold
for a very majestic soul
who's learned that each long night
has a morning after.

・・❋❋❋・・

Lesson 137:
Know your Worth

There is no need to twist your neck to watch your back when you can trust your own intuition.

So sometimes you might choose to carry others on your shoulders to help them reach a higher position.

And sometimes you might choose to hold others in your arms to help nurture their dreams into fruition.

But never allow your back to be confused with a foot stool—not ever under any condition.

And never allow your neck to be confused with a rung on a ladder that only leads to someone else's ambition.

Just be very clear
that you are here
as an equal child
of the Highest God
and you, too, are here
on a divine mission.

Lesson 138:
Guardian of God's Fruits

Even if you choose not to give your life to a partner; even if you choose not to allow your body to give birth—you still can choose to give life to others by offering them a sense of hope and a sense of self-worth.

So let your gentle hands nurture those who need love most. Let your generous heart beat rhythms that inspire.

Give encouragement and warmth to souls trying to find their way. Let love be both your food and your fire.

For the soul of a woman is the guardian of God's fruits. She is the protector of life and all of its essential truths.

Lesson 139:
Maternal Love is Eternal Love

For the Moms who guided us
to here from the unknown
before God guided their souls back Home...

For the children we still carry
in our hearts and in our wombs
even though they've gone back Home too soon...

Some part of everyday feels like a Mother's Day,
a time for memories, gratitude and mourning.

It is a time to give thanks for blessings
we no longer can see and touch—
the blessings we long to hold again
because we still miss them so much.

It is wanting to be gently reminded
and needing to make it clearly understood—
that we are eternally entwined and bonded
by the deep connections of Motherhood.

In that connection between a mother and child,
it still is and it will always be
a sense of *you and me and eternity*.
One bond. One love. One destiny.

Lesson 140:
A Peace of Her Soul

The time has come for the soul of a woman to be at the forefront of a peaceful revolution. The Creator is demanding that she share her understanding of creation, love, loss, and evolution.

So she no longer must sit in silence with folded hands and muffled cries. And she no longer must swallow as truth, what her conscience knows to be lies.

A woman's soul can see that God's sweetest fruits from Her garden are being devoured by the greedy jaws of war and the karmic return of fate.

And a woman's soul can hear that she is being called to mend 7 billion pieces of God's Heart to reclaim the Planet of Love from the jaws of hate.

For in order to evolve
to the next level of our humanity,
we must till the soil
and unearth the turmoil
to stop all this human insanity.

But the time for peace is now. And the soul of a woman must have a voice in that mission and a healing hand on that plow.

…because God has already shown her how.

Perfecting the Dance

Lesson 141:
May You Dance, Dr. Maya

Like a stream daring to flow alongside the River Nile—you made us feel greater; your strength made us smile.

So I thought that you'd stay with us for an even longer while—sharing your wisdom, your candor, your humor, your style.

But none of us knows our final day, nor can we see the final hour. So you taught us that, however long she's here, a woman must own her power. And you were more than just a woman: you were a guiding light from a mighty tower.

So may you rest in Poetry.
And may you rest in Peace.
And may you rest in knowing
that your words will never cease.

And may you dance with poets.
And may you dance with kings.
And may you dance like an un-caged hummingbird,
as all the Angels sing.

For while you will always be
remembered across eternity
as the dear and daring Dr. Maya Angelou—
the Heavens have called you back Home,
where you are known
as their very own:
Maya-Angel.

Lesson 142:
V Stands for Woman

A Woman is gonna do
what a girl has gotta do
when she wants to grow into
a Woman.

A Woman does not bow down and wait around—serving only as a bent spine for others to climb toward their dreams, while she is merely mounted.

When a girl sits, and the Woman inside her stands, Love becomes her pedestal, for finally she understands that her voice and her vision must also be counted.

So V stands for Woman and V stands in victory
because V has a vision and V has a voice.

Lesson 143:
Little Ms. BaddAzz

She may not start a fight but she knows very well how to end one. And she may not break the rules but she's been known to try to bend one.

She's not waiting to be dragged along or trampled on—not in anyone's wildest dreams. She knows how to set boundaries and build bridges and can push an envelope to its extremes.

Perfecting the Dance

She owns no rose-colored glasses. She likes her roses real because she respects each thorn. And she has been here, trying to look out for you, ever since the day that you were born.

She doesn't worry about the future, nor does she regret very much about the past. She lives fully in the present moment, seizing each second as though it were the last.

And while the others settle for "at least" she recognizes it as a concession that is far beneath "at best." So she expects good things from your life, for your life, and she frowns upon anything less.

Who on earth is she—this defiant, self-reliant, little Ms. BaddAzz chick—who defies social norms but then conforms to what makes you tick?

She is your "id"—your Inner-Diva. And she lives and loves freely from a place deep inside. And no matter how much you grow, or wherever you go, she likes tagging along for the ride.

So while you may try to keep her at bay, be sure that you give her a safe and warm place to play. And never permanently send her away—because she is a part of you, unfiltered and uncut. She is the one who waits around, who will lay things down, to pick you up.

And when your heart breaks, or you make mistakes, or even when you fall, she's the one inside willing to fight for your survival, any time you call.

And she, too, is God's gift to you.

Dr. Nesha Jenkins-Tate

Lesson 144:
Meditation: Ain't too Proud to Pray

There was a time when I thought the only time we should call on God was for life-threatening situations. The rest of the stuff, I believed, were matters we were well-equipped to handle on our own.

With all the monumental problems in the world, I didn't want to be a bother to God about random foolishness. So I bristled when people asked for prayers for things that seemed selfish, shallow, material or reasonably attainable if they only were willing to get up off their knees and roll-up their sleeves to work for it.

And there were also, I suppose, elements of distrust and impatience. I didn't want to risk asking for something that I wanted really badly and then have that thing not show up in my life just when I needed it most—for then I'd be left feeling that even God had let me down. And to whom then could I turn?

I didn't want God to see me as someone "weak" who spent more time on my knees than on my feet.

…But are we not weakened without faith?

I didn't want God to see me as just so "strong" that he might ask too much of me and I might do something wrong.

…But are we not able to do all things asked through our Creator who strengthens us?

Sometimes I didn't want God to see me at all. If I asked for nothing, then perhaps nothing would be asked of me. So I offered prayers that gave sincere thanks and I lived under the radar in a comfort zone that was my own little peaceful home.

…But what can hide us from a God who lives inside us?

And then finally, some things I didn't pray for simply because I knew in my heart that I was not emotionally and spiritually ready to receive them. I didn't believe myself worthy.

…But God knows our hearts, too, even before we do.

Thoughts such as these are the thin fantasies of the living dead. I celebrated my independence but truth is, my pride was standing between me and my faith.

The day that we proclaim ourselves indeed fully alive is the day that we finally realize that each breath is a gift and each day is a blessing. And all that is asked is that we respect life's plan and share our blessings and gifts as best we can—not in a spirit of perfection or even excellence, but in a spirit of love.

And let us never ever become too proud to pray—for strength, for guidance, for forgiveness, for love, for any and all things we cannot do on our own.

For prayer is a divine reminder that we are never alone.

Dr. Nesha Jenkins-Tate

Lesson 145:
Affirmation: I am a Soldier

I am a soldier of Love.
And today I'm being deployed
beyond my comfort zone.

But my ammunition is faith.
My intuition guides me
across terrains unknown.

I am on a mission to set free
every prisoner I see
bound by hate and fear.
Because my marching orders come
from deep inside me—
where the instructions are very clear.

I am a terminator of strife.
I am a protector of life.
I am a soldier of Love.

NOTES

NOTES

Chapter 13

The Choreographer of 7 Billion Dancers

·•✵✸✵•·

*God isn't dead and He isn't in hiding.
He didn't stop talking, listening, seeing and guiding
when scribes put down their sacred pens
some thousands of years ago.
He remains eternally alive and is actively in the flow.*

·•✵✸✵•·

*We need not be perfect
to give life our best—
because Love is the answer
whenever life gives the test.*

Chapter 13
The Choreographer of 7 Billion Dancers

Lesson 146: 7 Billion Pieces of God's Heart
Lesson 147: Falling on My Face and into Grace
Lesson 148: Ordering your Footsteps
Lesson 149: Many Seekers, Many Paths, One Destiny
Lesson 150: Pressing toward a Higher Mark
Lesson 151: Grieving the Loss from a Gold Mine
Lesson 152: All that Ever Is
Lesson 153: Same Blood
Lesson 154: Our Race toward Disgrace
Lesson 155: Words Unheard by the Elephants
Lesson 156: Meditation: Prayer of Humility
Lesson 157: Perfecting the Dance

Lesson 146:
7 Billion Pieces of God's Heart

The world was not created to be a heartless, mindless maze—
littered with human carnage trampled by the feet of greed and rage.

Our lives are sacred.
We share a goal.
The sum of our hearts
brings meaning to the whole.

And we were sent here, by design,
to share this appointed space and time,
that we might learn to come together
to channel Love and honor Grace.

And there is something,
both soothing and sobering,
that every human heart must come to face:

For even as we hurt and kill each other,
in a world grown closer yet falling apart,
we still are only 7 billion pieces
of our Divine Creator's heart—
sent here to resemble and to re-assemble
His Divine Love in this earthly place.

So let's find the time and the courage.
Let's seek the faith and the grace.
Let's search the wonderful colorful span
of our Creator's awesome face.

Dr. Nesha Jenkins-Tate

Then let's each ask ourselves how
we can begin now to do our part—
to help each other to stop the madness
that is breaking our God's Heart.

Lesson 147:
Falling on my Face and into Grace

There is a busy street-block downtown that I walk through some evenings after work, on my way to catching the subway train home.

Some days, about 30 men gather along that block, loitering in front of the library or the church, sometimes standing in line at a food-truck to get free meals.

I feel compelled here to say that I am not a snob; that actually, instinctively, I'm a social egalitarian. But seeing so much hopelessness in so many men in one space makes me feel uncomfortable and vulnerable as a woman.

I guess I see these men and then I see the roles I believe they should be serving with their lives—without also seeing human beings who may be merely trying to survive.

Sometimes, someone will ask whether I can spare any change. And always, avoiding eye-contact, I say, "Sorry, I can't."

You see, as a rule of thumb, I won't open my purse in the presence of strangers asking for money. And because I pass through this area frequently, I don't want to create an expectancy.

Perfecting the Dance

But one day as I was passing through, a man sitting on the church-step asked me whether I could spare some change. I responded the usual way. Then he said something that made me stop and look in his direction.

He said, "Even if you can't spare any change, I'd appreciate just a smile. Did you know that a smile can really touch somebody's heart?"

Wow.

Actually, I do know that. I guess I'd just forgotten that he and all the others were "somebody."

He wasn't flirting or scheming to get money. He was just one human being asking another for a smile. And it made me stop and look at him.

He had kind eyes. We exchanged smiles. And in that moment, I connected with him as another human being.

Ever since, it has been our ritual. Some days if he's on the other side of the street, he'll yell: "Hey, do I get a smile today?" And I deliver. It's our thing.

One day, as I passed him sitting on the ground, I said: "Hey, I've got a salad from lunch that I didn't have time to eat. Do you want it?" And he smiled and graciously accepted it.

Weeks later, I begged him to please take a red-velvet cupcake, admitting I'd cheated on my diet by buying two. Heck, I'd cheated by buying even one! And he laughed and said he'd help me out.

So now, I'm going to ask you to flash forward with me, in that same setting, to some weeks later.

I am a lady who likes dressing-up in high heels. But I also can be a very preoccupied lady, prone to clumsiness. I've fallen probably at least four times over the past year alone.

So it's gotten to the point now that I'm not even embarrassed about it anymore. I just get up, dust off, gather my stuff, and keep on walking—feelings and knees badly bruised, but head held ever so high. And, why not? Falling down is something that I do quite well!

Well, one day while waiting to cross a busy street in that homeless-zone, I lost my footing, fell off the curb, onto my knees and into the street. I and all of my belongings splattered in every direction.

Graceful? Clearly not.

But here's the thing. Several of those homeless men ran over and helped me to my feet, gathering my belongings and asking with genuine concern whether I was okay.

Humbling, to say the least.

While to this day, I still will not give them money, I will offer a piece of fruit if I have it and I will give eye-contact, a hello and, always, a smile.

In return, they have given me kindness, wisdom, humility and a little more human grace.

Perfecting the Dance

Lesson 148:
Ordering Your Footsteps

Order is perhaps the most fundamental law of Nature. It brings its own rhythm, sometimes even its own rhyme—for Order is a cosmic sequencing of things across space and time.

Music.
Math.
Karma.
Community.
Unity.
Law.
Awe.
Faith.

Beauty.
Balance.
Truth.
Prayer.
Apology.
Forgiveness.
Mercy.
Grace.

All are among the instruments in this earth-space, divinely designed to help us maintain order in this place.

Because when things feel out-of-order, life can be known as a living hell. But order creates peace in the spaces where chaos is prone to dwell.

So when chaos visits, threatening the quality of your life, remember that you were not placed here to live in constant agony and strife.

Remember that we've been granted many divinely powerful Instruments of Peace—and each is guided by laws that flow from the Love that will never cease.

Lesson 149:
Many Seekers, Many Paths, One Destiny

Some of us reside most comfortably in our Bodies. So we likely will be guided through movement, breathing and stillness.

Some of us reside most comfortably in our Hearts. So we likely will be guided by acts of courage and gifts of service.

Some of us reside most comfortably in our Minds. So we likely will be guided by the wisdom of thought-leaders and spiritual teachers.

Some of us reside most comfortably in our Souls. So we likely will be guided by the messages of prophets, poets and preachers.

But ultimately, no matter where we reside,
nor what we might choose as our guide,
we all will eventually arrive
at God's feet.

Perfecting the Dance

Lesson 150:
Pressing toward a Higher Mark

My heart refuses to re-calibrate
to the rhythm of a drum
that summons people to hate.

And my watch refuses to sync with the ticking beat
of people marching across time on backward feet.

So wherever I go, I go with the flow of life.

And life moves onward,
asking living souls to press forward,
inclining all to boldly lean toward
the highest call
of Love.

·•❋❋❋•·

Lesson 151:
Grieving the Loss from a Gold Mine

Dear God,
Please uplift our heavy hearts,
so burdened by the weight
of so many painful questions.

God, how can "We the People"
love our bullets and our guns—
even more than we can
love Your own daughters and sons?

Dr. Nesha Jenkins-Tate

How many children across the world will need to die?
How many traumatized families will need to cry
because blood that they love has been lost and found
as our homes, temples, schools, streets and land
become battleground?

And in the wake of her child's untimely death,
when someone who once shared her very breath
is suddenly and senselessly no longer there,
how does a mother exhale all that emptiness,
all that despair?

God, how does a wounded father channel his pain
into a higher purpose—so that no one's child again
has to be prematurely returned
to the heavens above?

And how does a community find comfort,
sifting through the ashes of chaos to heal—
so that one day again they might actually feel
that they can protect Your youngest
foot-soldiers of Love?

God, I know the answers to these questions are not hard—
unless the Guns have now become our new God.

Lesson 152:
All that Ever Is

Tearing down people's core beliefs
and leaving them truthless
is neither wise nor enlightening.
It is thoughtless and ruthless.

But God:

Cannot be carved into words covering walls
that separate our world religions...

Cannot be settled and won
by mental sparring and debate...

Cannot be confined
by the boundaries of human understanding...

Cannot be captured
in a gun-shell or a nutshell
by the language of hate...

So who are we,
the souls who march across human history,
who dare to stake our lofty claims

to declare sole-ownership
over a Creator and Sustainer
so often called by so many names?

We are the souls that God chose to live.

Dr. Nesha Jenkins-Tate

So perhaps He understands
and perhaps She forgives
because God forever, still,
and eternally is

…ALL…

Lesson 153:
Same Blood

When there is the opportunity for healing
that ultimately would benefit
the whole—

So foolish is the man
who, with razorblade in hand,
would scrape away the scab, in a selfish demand

To see if it will bleed the same color blood
that flows through the heart of
every soul.

Lesson 154:
Our Race toward Disgrace

Across the world, across time, across the world's great religions, we have grossly misinterpreted Scriptures that were sacredly written in the distant past. And we've used our religions to justify social-constructs that divide, diminish and dominate people based on skin and caste.

We have become disgracefully comfortable defining the worth of human beings based on "race" and matters of light and dark skin—when the spiritual Truth of the matter is actually a measure of the degree of Light (or darkness) that each person carries inside the Soul deep within.

The more we absorb of the Divine, the brighter our internal lights will shine, and the more we are able to see the beauty across and within all mankind.

Each soul experiences its own re-birth as it evolves and begins to channel toward this earth more of God's glorious Light. For it is the enlightened souls who help to uplift the human-race from the darkness of ignorance into an enlightened state—where we can embrace our divineness by transcending our divisiveness, our fears and wars, and even our hate.

Thus, the truest measure of beauty, of brilliance, of character is one's level of consciousness. It is a measure of enlightenment and it has nothing to do with race, skin-color or hue—but it has only to do with Love.

Only crayons identify themselves and each other through a label called "color." So let's step outside this crayon box and learn to like and love each other. We are not wax figures in a box, or still figures in a wax museum. We are 7 billion living, breathing, laughing, loving human beings... sent here merely to share the Love.

So let's set aside the lies and step inside the Truth. We are living in social disgrace. And the time has come to face and embrace the Light.

··•❄︎❉❄︎•··

Lesson 155:
Words Unheard by the Elephants

350 years
of a lucrative industry that caged its own species and told them what to do—toward producing bloody wealth for a self-righteous greedy few.

100 years
of witnessing one's own mankind choked to death by the ignorance of Jim-Crow—leaving watchful eyes trying to figure-out who to trust and where to go.

50 years
of a shared peculiar freedom, trapped inside an invisible cage, like an elephant disregarded by its herd—captured then by its own rage, held in bondage by unspoken words.

So today, let's sit here
caged together, and get clear,
in sober if sudden clarity of the magnitude and the travesty of that human timeline—one that is haunting to the human spirit and equally baffling to the human mind.

Perfecting the Dance

For all that God has ever asked is that we love ourselves and all mankind. And yet we fail Him daily, repeatedly, currently—across the globe and across time.

So for over 500 years in humanity's complicated life, we've remained scarred by mutual residual distrust and strife—carrying in our trunks the guilt, greed, hate, needs, shame, blame and pain of dead people who will never walk this earth again.

And yet, those old weary souls just seem to linger, darting in and out of living hearts like thorns between some swollen fingers.

And some souls linger to be forgiven.
And some just linger to be set free.
Yet elephants who live hopelessly in darkness
cannot forget the past because they cannot see.

So maybe somebody just needs to say:
"I'm sorry."

And maybe somebody needs to say:
"I'm done."

And maybe somebody can say:
"Let's kneel and heal together."

And maybe somebody else will say:
"We belong to One."

And maybe then everybody can say thank you, while asking God to help us to see our way through the looming, lingering spirit of the bad and sad things.

Dr. Nesha Jenkins-Tate

And maybe then all the elephants will draw near, as the dust of old spirits passes and things become clear.

And maybe then we'll all be able to see beyond fear, finally also willing to hear how we can free each other and fly together, even with these wounded wings.

Lesson 156:
Meditation: Prayer of Humility

God of the beginning and no end;
of things before and things again;

God of all genders and all people;
of the mosque, temple, church,
shrine, tent, and the steeple;

God of birth on this earth; of life and death;
of the breath-taking moments and the gift of breath;

God of the last planet and the first
and every star in the whole Universe;

God of everything that lives
and verily all that ever is—

I surrender myself humbly to Your Guidance.

Lesson 157:
Perfecting the Dance

It is in the moments when we feel most heart-broken that we are actually most spiritually open to the powerful healing energy of Love and Light.

Self-doubt can be that open door through which we invite the Creator to pour His Light to remind us of who we are in our core.

When soul-searching leaves us feeling unsettled;
when knees buckle where certainty ends—
I believe, my friends, that that is when
we have the chance to be awakened again.

The journey toward perfecting the dance
can then begin...

And the body will ask: WHAT?
And the mind will ask: WHY?
And the heart will ask: WHO?
And the soul will ask: HOW?

And we will remember that we are here,
and that here will always be WHERE.
And we'll remember that we only have now,
and that now is always WHEN.

And maybe, then:

When we can open-up to see just what might be our highest destiny... When we can grow to know just why we've been called to this stage of history... When we can embrace who we are, just as we are, loving ourselves unconditionally... When that ripple of Love spans across and above the ancient ponds of time and space... When it expands our embrace and we even find space to include the whole human race...

Perhaps it is then
that we are blessed again
to see the only face

who can choreograph perfection
into each dancer's role,

who can breathe new life and meaning
into every living soul,

who can allow each dancer's journey
to gracefully unfold

into

How.

NOTES

NOTES

Epilogue

Writers' Woes

Poets and writers
can be sensitive, porous and prickly.
Some say, perhaps, we merely are
as we were intended to be—
in order to openly channel
the seemingly random flow of energy
that pours into our souls,
across our hearts,
and through our pens.

But then again,
what an odd-fellow sometimes
I know that I can be
to the faithful friends and family
who know and love me.

Because living open to the word-flow of the Universe
is both a wonderful blessing and a bit of a curse.

It is a peculiar brand of vulnerability,
where there is a song, a poem, a feeling, a story
in nearly everything you see—
just waiting to be told by some opened soul
called here to set the rhythm of their voices free.

Dr. Nesha Jenkins-Tate

So some days, amid the craze of all these voices,
I just long to sing a song to set myself free,
to live a simpler life
on the outskirts of all this lunacy,
which I guess would be
to abandon the call of my own legacy.

But then again,
without my pen,
just who on earth would I be?

So from my heart and soul,
I write…

Afterword

There's something awesome about surviving the heart's rough and tumbling years through the teens, twenties, thirties and forties—even perhaps witnessing and surviving a glimpse of one's own mortality.

It can help you to arrive in the second half of your life feeling mercifully blessed and wise. It can bring you to a humble place of gratitude where you feel compelled now to decide that you must share all the gems you still might be carrying deep inside—even as you remain open still to learning more.

That's certainly how I feel right now: well-seasoned, worthy, and ready to share some lessons that recall much of the wit and wisdom earned and learned across a lifetime, thus far.

Perfecting the Dance is a book that was probably at least 15 years in the making. I felt moved to begin working on it just weeks after completing my doctoral studies. But at that time, I was struggling with extricating my authentic voice from the sometimes lofty language of academia. I felt so overwhelmed then by the possibility of another round of soul-searching, scholarly research and rigor, frequent all-nighters, and then facing yet more human scrutiny—that I ran away from the project in total horror!

Yet, in my heart of hearts, I have always been a writer and a poet—and one who has found the most wonderful muses and metaphors in the realm of dance. I see each of us in our life-walk as a dancer, on a planet now occupied by over seven billion of us.

I've probably been a poet since before I could read, write or spell. It is my calling.

I experience life as patterns, rhythms and cycles and I tend to express myself with candor and poetic cadence. Yet, I'm a pragmatist. So I wanted to write poetry not just for the self-indulgent sake of the poetry itself; not just for words to mingle among themselves being clever, rhythmic and beautiful; but for words that offer themselves as meaningful and useful to the everyday living experience of human beings.

So I guess I've always known my calling but I struggled to identify its higher purpose, a way that it might be most useful to the human experience.

My life's highest purpose is to create peace and harmony out of chaos; to create systems and rhythms, order and grace—within and across the human space.

As a hobby, it manifested itself early-on in my love of interior decorating and home-making. I still can recall some of those lovely little crawl-space cardboard homes I built in our backyard as a child. As a profession, for many years now, it has manifested itself in my services as a project management professional. Yes, I know. In this context, these both might sound incongruous or even rather mundane and trite, but there really is some synchrony.

While I might have neglected my highest calling (being a poet) for long stretches in my life, I believe I've always served my purpose (creating peace and harmony out of chaos) in

Perfecting the Dance

ways that felt safe for me at the time. Sometimes we have to be patient with ourselves as we expand our capacity for courageous service.

Five years ago, as my son headed off to college and I was no longer a year-round basketball-mom, this book started growing inside me again. By then, I felt rested and ready to write more seriously. I realized, however, that I am not a story-teller per se. And yet, I knew that there was a lot that I wanted to share, that I also felt called even to say, about some of the life-lessons learned on my journey along the way.

And more importantly, I knew that sharing those lessons might be useful and insightful to someone else.

Then the words inside me started to surge so strongly that they sometimes awakened me with a sense of urgency in the middle of the night. They came with such intensity that I knew that I had to summon the courage to give them a voice that could be heard broadly beyond me—even as I still struggled with the commitment required to give birth to a book of long form.

By then, we also had the powerful global forum of online social networking. So as I juggled a personal life, a professional life, and writing into the wee hours of the night, social networking became the outlet that allowed me to take baby-steps by publishing a daily blog. And daily, over the past several years, I've blogged on inspirational life-topics for an audience that has grown to thousands of new friends across the globe.

I've shared essays, testimonials, affirmations, poetry, prose, prayers and little epiphanies. Some days the words come forth, finding their way onto table napkins; into the margins of magazines; and inside the inked palm of my left hand. Once they even spilled onto my bed sheets as I could not find my notebook in the darkness. Then they are refined and presented daily to a friendly audience who often confirms that the words are indeed timely, inspirational, healing and resonant to other life experiences so many miles away.

Perfecting the Dance is a selected compilation of those life-lessons and love-lessons, along with new selections written exclusively for the book. In this forum, I actually like calling them all "dance-lessons."

Indeed, God lends each of us guidance—through our intuition, our conscience, our calling, and our relationships—through every circumstance. And all of these blessings helped to shape the lessons that have informed this dancer's dance.

So keep on dancing with life as it comes your way—with love, faith, and courage.

Nesha
January 27, 2015
Washington, D.C., USA

About the Author

Nesha L. Jenkins-Tate, Ph.D., PMP, is a writer, speaker, poet and philosopher. She adheres to the school of thought that philosophy should serve in pragmatic ways to heal and transform the human soul, and to improve the human condition. Author of *The 10 Love Poems to Empower Young Souls,* she also publishes a daily inspirational blog to thousands of followers globally.

Nesha completed undergraduate studies in Journalism at Howard University; a Master of Science from The Johns Hopkins University Carey Business School; and a Doctor of Philosophy from the Howard University Graduate School of Arts and Sciences. She serves as a program director in the health and wellness industry.

As a poet, a project management professional, and an inspirational speaker, "Dr. Neeesh" inspires people to find peace and harmony within and among themselves—as they strive toward serving their purpose while also achieving their goals.

Originally from the Sea Islands of Charleston, S.C., she currently lives in the Washington D.C. area.